## Additional Praise

"When I first heard this story presented by Miss Christopher at Findley Elementary, it really drew me in. Now being able to see it become a book is truly amazing! It is such an interesting story that can now be shared everywhere for a long time."
—Madison Keoouthai, age 14, 8th grader at Southeast Polk Junior High School

"As a descendant of the Dells, I grew up hearing stories about their friendship with Sitting Bull and the Sioux Indians in the Dakota Territory long ago. This new book, with its depiction of settlers' life on the prairie, captures the spirit of those true tales and the importance of one family's good relationship with their Native American neighbors. I hope that the historical events described here will encourage readers to value the lives of their own ancestors and be open to the experiences of other people different from themselves."
—Sharon Hudgins, author, journalist, and great-granddaughter of George and Lizzie Dell

# Our Friend Sitting Bull

## The True Story of a Pioneer Couple's Friendship with the Famous Lakota Chief

Mary R. Christopher

Ice Cube Press, LLC (Est. 1991)
North Liberty, Iowa, USA

*Our Friend Sitting Bull: The True Story of a Pioneer Couple's
Friendship with the Famous Lakota Chief*

Copyright ©2021 Mary Radcliffe Christopher

First Edition
ISBN 9781948509275

Ice Cube Press, LLC (Est. 1991)
1180 Hauer Drive
North Liberty, Iowa 52317 USA
www.icecubepress.com | steve@icecubepress.com

All rights reserved.

No portion of this book may be reproduced in any way
without permission, except for brief quotations for review,
or educational work, in which case the publisher shall be
provided copies. The views expressed in *Our Friend Sitting Bull*
are solely those of the author, not the Ice Cube Press, LLC.

The paper used in this publication meets the minimum
requirements of the American National Standard
for Information Sciences—Permanence of Paper for
Printed Library Materials, ANSI Z39.48-1992.

Manufactured in USA using recycled paper.

This book depicts actual events in the lives of the author's
great-grandparents and their friend, Sitting Bull, as truthfully
as family history permits and/or can be verified by research.
Occasionally, dialogue or thoughts consistent with the character or
nature of the person have been supplemented. All persons in the
story were actual individuals; there are no composite characters.
Any factual errors are inadvertent and those of the author.

The author can be contacted at OurFriendSittingBull@gmail.com

## DEDICATION

To my Great Grandparents, Lizzie and George Dell.
And to their friend, Tatanka lyotake, Chief Sitting Bull.
They shared a compassionate understanding of
human relationships.

Most of all, to the Dells' daughter, Ellen Dell Bieler, and
grand-daughter, Jean Bieler Hastings, who nurtured their
story for the generations to follow.

# TABLE OF CONTENTS

PREFACE ...... 7

PROLOGUE – THE DELLS AND THE LAKOTA (1863-1883) ...... 9

CHAPTER 1 – WESTWARD HO (1883) ...... 19

CHAPTER 2 – ARE WE THERE YET? (1884) ...... 24

CHAPTER 3 – SETTLING IN (1884) ...... 36

CHAPTER 4 – THE WILD WEST (1885) ...... 49

CHAPTER 5 – THE VISITOR (1886) ...... 60

CHAPTER 6 – YOUR FRIENDS ARE COMING (1887) ...... 78

CHAPTER 7 – DESSERT FIRST (1888) ...... 84

CHAPTER 8 – THE COWS AND THE KISS (1889) ...... 93

CHAPTER 9 – THE WORST YEAR EVER (1890) ...... 103

CHAPTER 10 – ALL THE DREAMS DIED (1891-1896) ...... 115

EPILOGUE – THE DELLS AND THE LAKOTA TODAY ...... 120

ACKNOWLEDGMENTS ...... 123

GLOSSARY ...... 125

BIBLIOGRAPHY ...... 128

ART AND PHOTO CREDITS ...... 129

QR CODE AND MORE INFORMATION ON THE DELLS ...... 131

# PREFACE

This is the true story of Elizabeth (Lizzie) and George Dell, a newlywed pioneer couple, and their unlikely friendship with the famous Lakota Sioux American Indian, Chief Sitting Bull. Their story began in 1883 when the future **homesteaders** married and then journeyed from northeastern Iowa to the westernmost part of the **Dakota Territory** to claim their new land.

By 1886, George and Lizzie met Sitting Bull. The Dells and Sitting Bull became friends even though they spoke different languages and came from almost completely different cultures.

Their friendship grew against the backdrop of the United States (US) Government's invented concept of **Manifest Destiny**. White people were given former American Indian lands, and American Indians were first encouraged, and later forced, to live on government-established Indian **reservations** that became increasingly smaller over time. The reservations tended to be in poor geographic areas where it was challenging to grow crops and feed livestock.

Sitting Bull resisted the White man's efforts to take away traditional American Indian lands and change the way the Indians lived. He stubbornly fought to keep alive his people's Lakota Sioux ways of life.

He once said, "The life my people want is a life of freedom. I have seen nothing that a White man has, houses or railways or clothing or food, that is as good as the right to move in the open country and live in our fashion."

But eventually Sitting Bull was forced to move to Standing Rock Reservation, which straddled the border between present-day South Dakota and North Dakota.

Biographies of him report that Sitting Bull was occasionally allowed to leave the reservation to travel as a celebrity in staged Wild West shows or to meet with US government officials.

Additionally, the **reservation agent** allowed Sitting Bull and his people to leave the reservation and roam the Dakota and Montana Territories many times a year as the **nomadic** people they were. They set up their tipis [tee-pees], rode their horses, hunted deer and elk, sharpened their knives and hatchets, and smoked their pipes.

Sitting Bull and his followers continued to trade as they always had, for example, deer meat and handcrafted **moccasins** were traded for clean well water and home-cooked meals. They even discovered desserts, which they loved to eat first, before the main course of meat and potatoes.

This small group of Lakota and their trusted chief continued moving in the open country and living in their fashion whenever they could, until Sitting Bull's death in December of 1890.

Given Sitting Bull's famous distrust of White people, it seems improbable that he would befriend Lizzie and George Dell. However, together this trio built a unique relationship that bridged their cultures. This is the true story of their friendship.

# PROLOGUE - THE DELLS AND THE LAKOTA (1863-1883)

In 1863, Elizabeth Halweg was born in Prussia (a mixed Germanic-Slavic region that historically belonged to both Germany and Poland), and immigrated to America with her parents and siblings in 1867. After eight years in New York City, the family decided to move to the Midwest and begin farming. A company had been formed in New York to purchase land in Howard County, Iowa; this may have been how the family learned of farming opportunities in Iowa. In 1875, when Lizzie was twelve years old, the family settled on a 360-acre farm near Davis Corners, Iowa—a German settlement located eleven miles west of Cresco, Iowa.

Lizzie worked in the fields alongside her brothers, plowing corn, pitching hay bundles, and helping with other chores. In the winters, she assisted a neighbor with household chores for $1 a week. She was expected to wash heavy farm clothes, iron, clean house, and help care for growing children.

Her future husband, George Dell, was already a young man of twenty years old at the time Lizzie was born. His family had purchased a farm in Howard County, Iowa when he was thirteen years old, and they moved there from New Jersey. George worked hard on the farm, taught school in a one-room schoolhouse (where some of the students were older than he was), and spent winters as a lumberjack in northern Wisconsin.

In 1865, George traveled to Illinois to enlist in the Union Army. It is not known why he joined an Illinois group, but his hometown was listed as Harlem, Illinois, just across the

Mississippi River from Iowa. He was initially stationed in Nashville, Tennessee where he soon became part of the 36th Illinois Infantry Regiment, Company 1, known as the Oswego Rifles of the Fox River Regiment. He later served as an Army **medic** in New Orleans, Louisiana. After his discharge back in Illinois, George reportedly walked the 350 miles back home to Cresco.

George resumed farming with his father, and in 1872 he purchased 160 acres of land for himself near Lizzie's family's farm, for $1,040, or $6.50 per acre. He built a small house on the land, planted trees, and farmed there for the next eleven years. During that time, his sister Adeline died at the age of thirty-three, leaving three young children, whom George then helped to raise.

No one could have predicted back in 1863 that, twenty years later, the baby girl and the Civil War soldier would unite in marriage near Davis Corners, Iowa, as Mr. and Mrs. George Dell—and move to the Dakota Territory to start a cattle ranch. And in their wildest dreams, the couple would not have believed that, once settled in the Dakotas, they would meet and befriend the most famous living Indian chief of their time, Sitting Bull.

In 1863, the same year that Lizzie was born, Sitting Bull was in his early thirties. The young Lakota **warrior** decided to visit his friends, the Santee Indians. The Santee had just been forced to move to a reservation at Crow Creek on the Missouri River in south-central Dakota Territory.

Sitting Bull was horrified when he arrived there. The ground was dry and barren and the water was not drinkable. He saw starving people, terrible illness, and many newly dug graves on the surrounding hills. He listened with sadness to the stories his Santee friends told him about how the White man had

Sitting Bull

driven them off their native land and how hard it was for them to adjust to this new land and new life.

Sitting Bull knew that, someday, the White man would similarly try to take away his beloved buffalo country. He vowed that when it happened, his heart would be strong and he would lead the fight against it to his dying breath.

AMERICAN INDIANS

The word "Indian" is used throughout this book because it was the term used during the time this story occurred. It comes from the much-earlier time of Columbus's voyages to North America (1490s), in search of a westward sea route from Europe to India and the Spice Islands. Columbus did not know that the North and South American continents lay between Europe and Asia, so when he reached land, he thought he had sailed to India. And he called the native people he met in that land "Indians"—even though they were actually the first people living on the North American continent.

Today, we generally use the term American Indians, First Nation (especially in Canada), or Indigenous (native) people. However, members of many American Indian tribes such as the Sioux prefer to be called by the name of their nation, for example, Lakota or Dakota.

In fact, it wasn't long before the White man began to take away his Lakota Sioux Indians' land and their rights.

At first the Indians did resist.

Chief Sitting Bull led this mostly peaceful resistance in the Dakota Territory. For several years he refused to cooperate with the White man. He refused to sign the White man's **treaties**. He refused to give more land away. He refused to give up.

In 1862, President Abraham Lincoln signed two acts into law. First, the Pacific Railroad Act gave millions of acres of land across the country to companies that planned to build railroads.

The Indians resisted.

They knew that the trains would frighten the herds of buffalo, deer, and elk that roamed the land. This would make hunting game much harder for the nomadic Lakota. But soon thousands of workers began building train tracks across the prairie.

Second, the Homestead Act of 1862 granted White (and freed Black) pioneers valuable pieces of land called homesteads. After living and working (farming or ranching) on the land for five years, the homesteader could obtain title to the 160 acres of land by paying the land office fees of $4 to $8 (the equivalent of $100 to $200 today). More than 270 million acres of public land—nearly ten percent of the entire US—became available to 1.6 million homesteaders.

The Indians resisted.

This time the various Sioux tribes along with the Cheyenne [shai·an] and Arapaho [a rap a-hō] decided that uniting together would strengthen their resistance, and they chose Chief Sitting Bull as leader over all of them.

In 1868, the US government drew up the Fort Laramie Treaty, which established the Great Sioux Reservation. The reservation was roughly the size of the state of Maine.

The Indians resisted.

But many moved to the reservation anyway because they were promised food, warm clothing, and the liberty to always roam the land. However, some of the Indians who refused to move there became known as Sitting Bull's people or Sitting Bull's followers because they wanted to continue to stay with their chief.

Soon, white gold miners from eastern states heard they might find gold in the **Black Hills** and they began to come there in droves.

The Indians resisted.

They believed the Black Hills to be a sacred place where the souls of their **ancestors** lived. Also, the Fort Laramie Treaty stated that White settlers were not allowed in the Black Hills because the hills were part of the Great Sioux Reservation. It didn't matter—the gold miners kept coming.

By the early 1870s, the gold miners reported to people in their home states back east that the area would be ideal for cattle ranching, because there was abundant grass and water to be found there. This attracted the attention of people who were involved in the beef cattle industry.

The Indians resisted.

They did not want even more White people moving onto their traditional lands. But the cattle ranchers came, along with their cowboys and horses and enormous herds of cattle.

By 1875, President Ulysses S. Grant was concerned about three thousand Indians in the area who still roamed free. He directed that all Indians in this part of the country must move to the Great Sioux Reservation.

The Indians resisted.

Those three thousand Indians included Sitting Bull and his 200 to 300 followers. They either did not hear about the President's order or they chose to ignore it. By February, the government sent armies to try to round up the "hostile Indians" who refused to move to the reservation.

Fighting broke out over the course of the next few months. Sitting Bull tried to avoid it by moving his followers to Montana Territory where they set up their camp in the valley of the Little Big Horn River. In June, they were attacked there by the Seventh US **Cavalry** [ka·vuhl·ree] led by **Colonel** [ker-nel] George Custer.

The Indians resisted.

In the months since the army had been tracking them and burning their camps, the Indians had built up their forces. Custer's 650-man army was quickly and soundly defeated by thousands of Indians. The Battle of the Little Bighorn has been called the most famous battle of the Indian wars in the history of the United States.

Custer died in the battle, but no one has ever been able to figure out who killed him. Sitting Bull was too old to still be a warrior at that time. He had reportedly taken charge of quickly getting the women, children, and elderly safely away from the battle and was believed to have been miles away when Custer was shot.

US government officials were very angry at the outcome of that battle. The Indians' defeat of Custer during the year of the United States' one-hundredth birthday in 1876 was the final blow. The government vowed to end what they considered the "Indian problem" once and for all.

The reservation Indians had their guns and horses taken away from them. The government hired special marksmen to shoot and kill all of the buffalo, sometimes from moving trains. Sitting Bull would later say, "A cold wind blew across the prairie when the last buffalo fell...a death wind for my people."

Still, the Indians resisted.

But their resistance was weakening. The **demise** of the buffalo was the end of the Indians' existence as they had always known it. Many more Lakota sadly moved onto the reservation.

Congress had drawn up a new document called the Indian Appropriations Act of 1876. This stated that the Indians had to give up the Black Hills and their hunting lands, or the government would not allow food to be sent to the reservations.

Again, the Indians resisted.

They thought this was an unfair act, but they eventually had to sign the document or they and their families would face starvation. The US had finally managed to steal the sacred Black Hills from the Indians. Years later, Chief Red Cloud said this was the only promise the White man ever made good on—to take the Indians' land away from them.

Sitting Bull and an estimated 200 to 300 of his followers moved across the border to Canada to avoid the reservation life. After about four years, the Canadian government told the group they must return to the US. They did, and were promptly arrested and held at Fort Buford in the Dakota Territory. Twenty months later, in 1883, they were finally escorted to Standing Rock Indian Reservation.

The White man had taken or ruined the Lakota's sacred lands, killed all the buffalo, and completely defeated the Indians and their ways.

Sitting Bull knew that the old Lakota ways of life were finally coming to an end. He decided he would embrace this new life as best as he could. He had to do this to keep his followers from starving to death and to ensure a future for his children.

He made up his mind to farm the land and raise cattle as the White people desired. He would live in a log cabin and dress in the White man's clothes when he had to. Sitting Bull's children would go to school to learn the White man's ways. He vowed that his children would learn English so they could get along in the White man's world.

Sitting Bull would resist no more.

But he despised the White people for killing the buffalo, forcing his Lakota followers onto reservations, and destroying their unique culture forever.

## CHIEF SITTING BULL?

Sitting Bull, although agreeable to the "Chief" title, was considered to be at a level higher than a chief as a medicine man / spiritual leader. Chiefs led multiple and various events, not people, and Indians did not have to follow a chief's leadership unless they wanted to. Chiefs were relied upon for their particular strengths; Sitting Bull's primary strengths were planning, negotiation, and influencing others under various circumstances, such as at the Battle of the Little Big Horn.

## THE BUFFALO OR BISON

A bison is actually a type of buffalo, but buffalo was the common term for bison in the United States in the 19th century.

A bull or male bison measures about fifteen feet from nose to tail, longer than most cars. He stands about seven feet high at his shoulder, as high as a doorway in a house, and he weighs about 2,500 pounds.

In 1831, when Sitting Bull was born, there were about forty to fifty million bison roaming the plains. In 1862 someone reported seeing a bison herd several miles wide, galloping by at about thirty miles per hour for over an hour. Some who saw the bison in those days said that there were so many bison they made the plains look like wall-to-wall, dark-brown carpeting.

The bison would move, or migrate, across the plains, searching for new grass to eat. The Lakota would pack up their tipis and their belongings and follow the bison to new hunting grounds.

The Indians depended on the bison for almost everything in their lives.

Bison meat was the Lakota's main food. The Lakota **tanned** the leather hide and made it into **robes**, clothing, and even new tipis. The Indian women scraped the bison hides using scrapers made from bison bones. The brains were used to tan the hides. **Sinew** [sin you] from the bison was used to sew tipis, clothing, and moccasins. The Indians cooked stew in a bag made from a bison's stomach. They placed meat, water, and roots in the bag and then cooked it by adding hot rocks to it. Much of the meat was dried for winter. Hollow horns became cups and spoons. Bones were shaped into digging tools. Hooves were used to make glue. Skulls were saved for ceremonies. Dried bison manure was used to build fires.

To force the Plains Indians onto the reservations, the US Government decided to get rid of the bison. Between 1872 and 1874 alone, marksmen hired by the government shot almost four million bison. Most of their bodies were just left to rot on the plains.

Of all the bison killed in that short time period, an estimated four percent (one out of every twenty-five) were killed by Indians and the rest were killed by white people.

The Sioux name for white man, Wasicus (wah see cooz), does not mean white or paleface like some people think. It actually means "the ones who take the fat." The white people generally took the meat of the bison (if they took anything at all) and left the rest. Wasicus meant "greedy and wasteful."

By 1896, after the Dells had returned to Iowa, there were fewer than 1,000 bison left in the entire US.

Since 1896 many people have worked hard to save the bison, bringing the animal back from near extinction. Today, the bison population is estimated at 500,000.

# CHAPTER ONE – WESTWARD HO (1883)

In April 1883, George Dell filed a claim for 160 acres of land in the Dakota Territory, near a town called Kimball. He traveled there mostly by train with his friend, George Lane, to choose the spot, and hired a local man to build a tiny cabin on the land. That summer, he returned to Cresco to propose marriage to Lizzie and to plan their trip west together.

George wanted to start a cattle ranch in the Dakotas. He had heard that this was a good way to make a living. Once Lizzie agreed to George's proposal, she became eager to have her own home and start a new family. Going west with her new husband would be a great adventure!

By that May, Sitting Bull and his followers were living on the Standing Rock Reservation. There they met James McLaughlin, the Indian agent, who was a tall, dignified man of Scottish descent. McLaughlin's wife, Marie, who was part Indian, was the official interpreter for the reservation.

Sitting Bull quickly found that living on the reservation was very different from living in a tipi. His log house, with its lack of sunlight and air flow, was dark and stuffy compared to his family's tipi. The land that he was given to farm was of poor quality, and the slow plow horses seemed boring compared to his beautiful warhorses. Instead of hunting elk and buffalo, he raised chickens and cattle. It was a completely different way of life that would take some getting used to.

To Sitting Bull's credit, he vowed to make a success of "living off the soil" on the reservation. His farm eventually had

Agent James McLaughlin

forty-five cows, eighty chickens, and twenty horses. He and his family grew corn, oats, and potatoes. They had sheds, haystacks, and an underground root cellar in which to store fruits and vegetables.

Soon, Sitting Bull wisely requested that the reservation's Indian agency build a day school near his cabin. That way, his children and those of his relatives and other followers could spend the nights with their families at home instead of living at boarding schools far away from the reservation. His request was granted, and a small school was built nearby. There, the Indian children would be taught to paint, cook, learn math, and speak English. They would also learn order, obedience, and habits of cleanliness from their White teachers.

Elaine Goodale, the founder of another day school on the reservation (and later the education supervisor for North Dakota and South Dakota), regularly came to check on the school near Sitting Bull's home. She later said that Sitting Bull was surely the "most famous living Indian chief." Even Agent McLaughlin agreed that Sitting Bull was "by far the most influential man of his Sioux **nation** for several years," and he claimed that none of the other Sioux chiefs had nearly the power that Sitting Bull did.

However, McLaughlin did not like Sitting Bull and frequently told him that he was no longer a chief. This angered Sitting Bull but, of course, Agent McLaughlin did not have the power to unmake an Indian chief. Also, no matter what McLaughlin thought of him, Sitting Bull's fame continued to spread across the country.

In September of 1883, the US government held a celebration for the opening of the Northern Pacific Railway. Sitting Bull was invited to make one of the speeches. The government officials hoped that his presence would prove to everyone that the Indians and the White people had become friends.

Sitting Bull wrote his speech ahead of time so his interpreter could translate it to English and submit it to government officials for approval.

On the special day, Sitting Bull joined former US President Ulysses Grant, the US Secretary of State, and many other notable figures who were in attendance at the ceremony. Although no one knows exactly what his original "approved" speech said, Sitting Bull obviously decided to change its message as he spoke. What he actually said that day would never have been pre-approved by the US government.

When his turn came to speak, he stood up and reportedly said, in his native Lakota language, "I hate all White people. You are thieves and liars. You have taken away our lands and made us outcasts." His interpreter quickly changed Sitting Bull's words into English, but turned the message into a friendly one for the crowd.

As Sitting Bull continued speaking, he went on to describe the terrible things that his Lakota people had endured at the hands of the US government. Between his statements, he paused to smile, and the audience cheered. He bowed in return and then continued his bitter speech. At the end, believing the chief had said nice things about White people, the crowd jumped to their feet and cheered wildly.

Lizzie and George were married on Saturday, November 17, 1883, in the living room of her parents' farmhouse near the town of Cresco, Iowa. The bride wore a long black dress, which was the custom at that time. A small, gold brooch, a gift from her father, was pinned on her collar. It was a short ceremony, and afterward the wedding guests stayed for supper.

Lizzie was twenty years old and George was thirty-nine. He had worked as a farmer for several years and had saved money for the future. He also had a friend in Cresco, the town's pharmacist (also a farmer who raised cattle), Dr. J.J. Clemmer, who wanted to invest some of his own money in the Dells' future cattle ranching operation.

The next few days were full of preparations for Lizzie and George's trip west to the Dakota Territory. Trunks and boxes were packed with necessities for the couple's new home. Their packing list included an all-purpose medical book (because there would be no doctors there), a calendar, two cookbooks, and Lizzie's Bible.

At noon the following Friday, family and friends all gathered at the Cresco railroad station to see them off. The couple's destination was the small town of Kimball in the Dakota Territory. From there they would travel by wagon to their new cabin nearby.

When they arrived in Kimball, a few miles east of the Missouri River, they were met at the train by George Lane—the friend who had helped George Dell locate a good homesteading spot the previous year.

Unfortunately, the Dells soon found out that the land claim George Dell had filed in April near Kimball was in dispute. They learned that a clerk had filled out the claim papers incorrectly and, because of the errors, someone else now owned the land.

George knew he had no choice but to sell his cabin to the new land owner, since the land was no longer his. In the meantime, the couple was invited to share George Lane's home in Kimball, with five cowboys also staying there, over the winter.

During this period, George Dell laid claim to another 160 acres, this time in a much less populated area in the far western part of the territory. This land, offered for sale by the US Government, had traditionally been part of the Sioux Indian lands, in an area of the Dakotas called the Cave Hills.

The Dells were excited to continue westward once the spring weather arrived.

# CHAPTER TWO -
# ARE WE THERE YET? (1884)

In March 1884, Sitting Bull heard that reservation agent James McLaughlin was planning a trip to St. Paul, Minnesota. The chief wanted to learn more about the ways of the White people, so he asked if he could go along. McLaughlin agreed.

The Northern Pacific Railroad provided free train tickets for Sitting Bull, one of his two wives, and his son, One Bull. McLaughlin's wife, Marie, accompanied the group to act as interpreter.

In St. Paul, Sitting Bull saw many things he had never seen before. He watched the printing presses of the St. Paul Pioneer Press newspaper, and he was in awe of a grocery wholesale warehouse with its endless shelves of food.

He toured all sorts of manufacturing facilities, including those that made coffee, cigars, clothing, boots, and shoes. At the shoe factory the craftsmen even made him a new pair of shoes.

When the group visited the local firehouse, Sitting Bull was delighted by everything he saw. He was especially impressed when the firemen demonstrated their quick response to a fire call. The alarm bell clanged and the firemen slid down the pole from their living quarters upstairs. They quickly hooked the horses up to the fire engines and off they went. Sitting Bull enjoyed it so much that he requested a repeat performance. This time the firemen let him start the clanging fire bell himself!

Meanwhile, back in Kimball, the Dells were preparing for their long journey to their new homestead site.

St. Paul Firehouse

They planned to first head west toward the Black Hills region of southwestern Dakota, and then travel north to the Cave Hills.

That April, the Dells had young **Black Angus** cattle shipped by railroad to Kimball from Cresco, Iowa. The cattle were **branded** "CCC"—most likely for Cresco Cattle Company—and would later become the Dells' first herd on their Triple-C cattle ranch.

George's own team of horses also came by train from Cresco. It was typical at the time for a man to have his own team of horses that he knew and trusted.

Before leaving Kimball, the couple purchased two covered wagons, food supplies, a kitchen alarm clock, some oxen, and several cow ponies, The cowboys would ride the small and agile cow ponies to keep the cattle herd together on the trip.

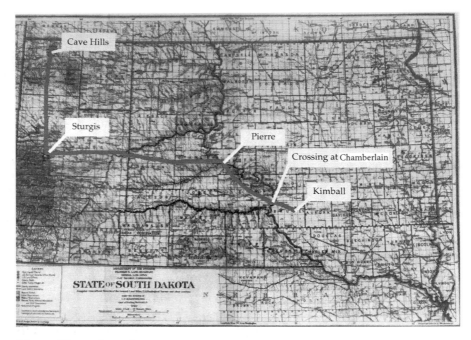

Map of travel route

Black Angus cows

Two of the cowboys traveling with Lizzie and George Dell were George Lane and George Lloyd, both from the Kimball, Dakota area—so, there were three Georges all together. The other two cowboys were John Flissam from Wisconsin and Frank Bothwick from Cresco, Iowa. It wasn't long before Lizzie began to call this small group of men her family.

On May 1st, 1884, the Dells began their journey.

Their first stop was the town of Chamberlain, where they had to cross the Missouri River. It was quite a challenge to bring the wagons down to the river ferry, as the river was fifty feet downhill from the town. Once they finally arrived at the river, it took two trips on the flat, wooden ferry to get everything across. The ferry boat captain took the cattle and cowboys across on the first trip; the horses, wagons, and the Dells went across on the second trip. The cost was about one dollar each for the two wagons, plus ten to fifteen cents for each person, horse, or cow.

The next leg of the trip involved traveling from Chamberlain to Fort Pierre [peer]. George drove one of their covered wagons which was pulled by oxen, while the cowboys, on their ponies, herded the cattle. Lizzie, now two months pregnant with their first child, drove George's team of horses that pulled the other covered wagon.

Since their journey required them to cross the lower Brulé [bru-lay] Indian Reservation, they'd had to obtain permission from an Indian agent in Chamberlain. The Dells found that a lot of Dakota land was made up of Indian reservations.

On the way, the group planned to stop at **trading posts** to buy enough **provisions** to get them to the next trading post.

When they arrived at the trading post in the town of Fort Pierre, Lizzie could not find her shoes in the back of the wagon. She was so thirsty that she could not wait to have a drink, so

River Ferry Crossing

she walked barefoot into the trading post with George, and they drank muddy Missouri River water from a barrel. It tasted heavenly!

The small group usually traveled from two to eight miles a day. Because they needed to spend each night near water for their cattle, there were some days they could travel only a few miles. The cowboys took turns riding ahead of the group to locate the next drinkable water source.

George, Lizzie, and the cowboys drank water from the creeks and puddle holes. The men typically filled a canteen for Lizzie. They tried to drink before the herd of cattle did because the water did not seem as clean after the cattle drank. When they couldn't find suitable water, the group opened canned tomatoes and drank the juice to stay hydrated.

They knew that a muddy puddle was safer to drink from than a crystal clear one, because a clear one was sure to contain

Typical Pioneers

**alkali**. One of the cowboys once drank from a clear puddle and became so sick he could not eat for several days. Bathing in a clear puddle could also result in a terrible skin rash. So, when the group found a muddy puddle, they would stop for the night. They boiled the water to remove impurities, and sometimes even made coffee with it.

The men would unload the small iron cookstove from one of the wagons and set it in a tent for Lizzie to cook dinner. The next day she would use the stove again to bake bread and cook breakfast.

Everyone ate an early breakfast in the mornings. This typically included coffee, homemade bread, fried bacon, and eggs or canned beans when available. After breakfast, the men scooped the fire out of the stove and allowed the stove to cool, then, reloaded the oven onto the wagon.

Once the men packed up the tents, the wagons always took off first to avoid being behind the cloud of dust churned up by the walking herd of cattle.

Since there were no fences on the land, the cattle had to be guarded at night to keep them from straying away. Two men were assigned this job from sundown to midnight. Two other men took over at midnight and guarded the cattle until sunrise.

Every other day, when the group stopped at noon to eat lunch, Lizzie would mix yeast and other ingredients for the next two days' bread. The dough would then rise during the day as they traveled.

At noon, they stopped to build a fire to cook their midday meal. Lunch typically included coffee, bread, bacon, and canned tomatoes. First, they placed two forked iron poles in the ground and set an iron rod across them. Then they hung a coffee pot from the iron rod over the fire and draped bacon over the rod to fry.

The fires were made by burning cow chips (dried cow manure) that Lizzie collected along the way in a burlap sack. Lizzie also used this same fuel to build fires to wash clothes for the group. They were lucky that it was a dry summer, or the chips would have been too wet to burn.

Lizzie wasn't the only one involved in the bread-making process. She always told the night-shift cowboys to wake her when the dough had risen "so high," gesturing with her hand. That usually happened around midnight. Upon waking, she would form the dough into loaves. The cowboys were then instructed to wake her again when it began to get light outside—between three and four o'clock in the morning—so Lizzie could start a fire. Then she baked the bread before the group hit the trail for the day.

Occasionally they traveled through wooded areas, but it took a long time to cut firewood and it was heavy to carry back to the wagons. For these reasons, cow manure was the fuel of choice.

Laundry day was usually once a week, on a day when the group stopped traveling early in the afternoon. Lizzie used a **washboard** to scrub the clothes and bedding. The water was heated over the fire, for washing and rinsing the laundry, and then cold water was thrown over the laundry to cool it down. Finally, the clean clothes were wrung out and hung to dry.

Washboard

The men would place the wagons parallel to each other and string clothes lines between them. Cotton items dried quickly, but wool items did not always dry overnight. Those would be folded and put in a box until they could be hung out again the next day.

The group traveled from Fort Pierre to the **Badlands** on the **stagecoach** road. Once they arrived, they found the Badlands to be a confusing area to traverse, because it was full of steep hills, deep valleys, and strange rocks that seemed slippery even when dry. Soon the group became lost and disoriented.

Badlands

When they came upon a lone Indian, the travelers were more relieved than afraid. George offered him a dollar to help guide them. Fortunately, the Indian was able to lead them to the one place that was wide enough for the covered wagons to leave the Badlands and head towards the group's destination. Otherwise, the men would have had to unload the wagons, take them apart, and carry everything out of the badlands by hand. So, everyone agreed the dollar was well spent.

One humid morning when they woke up, they noticed that the cattle were strangely restless. George said the cattle's nervousness meant there was a thunderstorm coming and, sure enough, the sky soon darkened. The cowboys hurriedly put up a tent wall next to the wagons for additional protection from the coming rain, because not everyone would fit inside the provision-laden covered wagons. Soon, the wind picked up and broke the pole that held up the tent wall. The tent wall fell and the rain was so torrential that even the bedding in the wagons got soaked.

Once the wind died down, the men put the tent wall up again to create shelter for the night. Three of the cowboys stood guard while everyone else crawled under the wet bedding still wearing their daytime clothes to keep warm. At about 1:30 in the morning, the men switched guards on duty so that the ones who had been watching the cattle could sleep for a while.

The next morning, the group continued west towards the trading post at the small settlement of Sturgis in the Black Hills. To reach Sturgis, they had to cross the Cheyenne River where there was no ferry service. The horses and oxen pulled the wagons through the water, which came all the way up to the tops of the giant wagon wheels.

Before they arrived in Sturgis, one of their milk cows gave birth to a calf. The group decided this would be a good time to stop for lunch and give the mother time to lick her new baby clean and nudge it to its feet.

After lunch, they continued on toward Sturgis. As they pulled out, the milk cow began to bellow. She suddenly could not locate her new calf. The mother cow continued to cry and moan while running back to where they had stopped for lunch in search of it.

Two of the men decided to follow the mother cow and saw that she ran to a farmer's barn. The men could not coax the mother away from the barn door, so they opened it and found the calf inside. Clearly, the farmer who owned the barn had

Fording the River

stolen the calf. Once mother and baby were reunited, the group went on its way. Making good travel time was more important than locating and punishing the thief.

They headed north through the Belle Fourche [foosh] area to the Cave Hills, their final destination. From a distance, the rugged **buttes** [byoots] ahead of them were a soft burnt-reddish color. The Cave Hills area was about twelve square miles in total area, with a pair of hills called North Cave Hill and South Cave Hill. The two hills looked as though they had suddenly popped up out of the prairie one day. Their perfectly-flat tops were covered with pine trees and grasses.

The travelers found the sides of the two hills to be from 25-to-100 feet steep, with only a few places where the wagons and the animals could get up and down the hills.

The group eventually came across Bull Creek, which flowed between North and South Cave Hills. They found an old rancher by the name of Gallup living along the creek, who claimed to have killed the last buffalo in the area. He had the buffalo hide stretched out on the ground with the fur side up and had cut the word "LAST" into it. Sadly, by the time George and Lizzie arrived in the Cave Hills the buffalo in the area were indeed entirely gone.

Gallup told them that four to five miles up Bull Creek would be a good place to start a cattle ranch. There were only four other cattle ranches in the entire twelve square miles of the Cave Hills, so it did seem like that would be a perfect spot. The fence-less area was too remote for most homesteaders to live on, so it offered ample grazing ground for the cattle.

The group headed upstream until they found the site that Gallup had described. They stopped and looked all around them in awe of its beauty.

The setting looked like a watercolor painting. The broad, blue sky was full of low-hanging, fluffy white clouds that softened the bright glare of the sun. Swaying tan and green prairie grasses were home to singing meadowlarks. A wonderful fragrance from low bushes of silver-green sage filled the air. The group spotted several antelope and deer beyond the winding Bull Creek.

It was the perfect site for their ranch.

At last their trip was over. It had taken them four months to travel the 400 miles from Kimball to the Cave Hills.

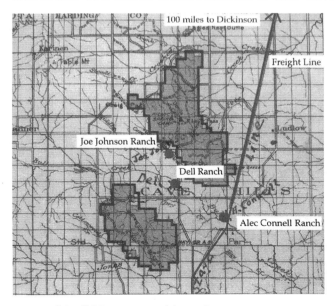

Map of Dell Homestead location

# CHAPTER THREE - SETTLING IN (1884)

The Dells would remain at this location for the next twelve years. And for most of that time Lizzie would be the only White woman within one hundred miles. The area was so remote she decided to return to Iowa to give birth to each of the four children born during the couple's twelve years as Dakota cattle ranchers.

When the Dell group first arrived in the Cave Hills area, the men quickly pitched a sleeping tent and everyone began unpacking the wagons to establish their first home. The Homestead Law required that they build their house within six months of claiming their land, so the men soon traveled into the hills to cut pine logs.

The couple's first house was a one-room log cabin, only 12-by-13 feet (about the size of today's average bedroom). It had a dirt floor and a roof most likely made of wood poles, hay, and sod. Holes were cut in the walls for two windows and a door. Later, a **freight wagon** from Dickinson, a hundred miles north of there, would bring glass for the windows and lumber for a door.

The freight wagon ran along the new stagecoach road between the towns of Dickinson and Deadwood.

The materials were unloaded from the freight wagon at the Gallup ranch, which was on the stagecoach road. Then, they were transported five miles by smaller wagons over rougher terrain to the Dells' cabin.

36

Eastern Hunters on Deadwood Medora Stagecoach

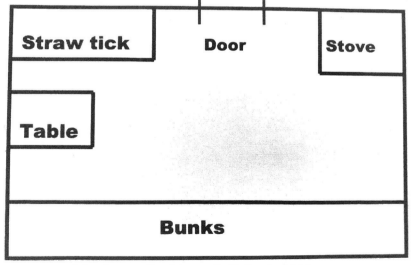

*Diagram of the first Dell cabin on Bull Creek, 1884*

The company that sent the lumber for the door forgot to include hinges, so George put up a pole to hold the door in place when it was closed. That way, the cattle could not wander in and, also, the door would not fall in on the men who were sleeping on the floor.

Inside the cabin, wood poles and boards were used as framework to build two raised beds against the wall. Those skinny beds, both the same height, allowed for storage of boxed clothing and canned goods below. Lizzie and George slept on one bed and two of the cowboys slept on the other.

While the men were cutting the wood with axes to build the cabin, one of them, John Flissam, nearly cut off one of his toes by accident. George took him by wagon to Gallop's ranch so John could catch the stagecoach to Dickinson to see a doctor. Unfortunately, they were too late and the stagecoach had already gone. There was nothing to do but take John back to the Dell ranch.

Once back at the cabin, George secured the toe in place and bandaged John's foot. Eight days later, when he soaked the bandage off, both men were surprised to find that the toe had healed.

As soon as the house was built, two of the men left the Dells' to "go back to civilization," as they called it. George Lane needed to return to his house in Kimball, where the group had begun their trip the previous May. Frank had a sweetheart back home in Iowa from whom he could no longer bear to be apart.

George needed more cowboys to help with the cattle, so he soon hired two young men who came through the area looking for work. A working cowboy at that time was generally paid $25 to $30 a month (about $625 to $750 in today's money), with free meals provided and also a straw-tick mattress or bed when he stayed overnight at the ranch.

The new men slept on a cotton-covered straw mattress on the floor. On cold nights they pulled the mattress close to the kitchen stove, and liked to stick their feet under the stove to keep warm. On mild evenings, they would drag the mattress outdoors and sleep under the stars.

When the Dells ordered the lumber for their new door, they also bought some extra planks, which the cowboys made into a table. For dining chairs, they sat on the wooden boxes that their canned goods came in.

Since the pine walls of the Dell cabin were natural wood, sticky resin sometimes oozed out of the logs. One morning

Bull Creek

Lizzie awoke and found that she was actually stuck to the bed because her hair was caught in the pine resin. George had to get the scissors and cut off some of her hair to get her loose.

Bull Creek ran in site of the cabin, a few dozen yards away. The group drank water from the creek upstream and dammed up some of the water to create a bathing pool downstream.

Because the cowboys lived in the tiny cabin with the Dells, certain rules were established to help Lizzie keep her privacy. When she dressed, all the men turned their faces towards a wall, with their backs to Lizzie. For bathing, everyone took turns heading down a steep bank to the creek, while all the others waited behind in the cabin.

Lizzie usually got to go to the creek first, and she always took a pail, soap, and a sponge with her. One day after she had bathed and then dressed in fresh clothes, she slipped and fell back into the creek! She got completely soaked and had to return to the cabin to find dry clothes and then bathe all over again.

Eventually, George and the cowboys dug a deep hole in the yard to create a well. The entire group was excited to have this new source of clean water so close to the house. However, when a skunk came too close to the house and George tried to ward it off with a long pole, the animal fell into the well and drowned. So, the group had to go back to drinking water from Bull Creek for several months while they scooped stinky water from the well and waited until it naturally filled itself with fresh water again.

The cowboys were highly respectful of Lizzie. They called her "Mrs. Dell" and were careful to never swear within earshot of her. And typical of manners at that time, Lizzie always called George "Mr. Dell" in front of the cowboys.

Other cowboys often came to the cabin. Some were men who were hired to work for only a short time, whereas others were cowboys who were just passing through that area. The Dells were very trusting, so they never locked their house. Trusting everyone, including strangers, was a normal part of pioneer life. Even if the Dells were not home, any cowboy could let himself in to cook and eat whatever he could find, usually baked biscuits and canned goods. The cowboy would then clean up if he had the time, or write a quick apology note if he did not.

Lizzie later said they never had a cowboy in the house who was not a complete gentleman. They always left their hats and their holsters with their **six shooters** in the fenced-in corral where the horses were kept. The cowboys spoke politely and always thanked Lizzie for her kindness when they left.

There was no time for laziness at the Triple-C Ranch. Everyone was constantly busy. George and the men cared for the cows and horses, maintained the horse corral and the house, and cut firewood. Lizzie cooked meals on her iron stove and baked bread for all the men. She kept everyone's clothes clean and mended, and she made soap, butter, and jams. She also set aside a little time every day to read her Bible.

The neighbors who owned the other cattle ranches in the Cave Hills were three unmarried men. Joe Johnson and his nephew Gene each owned their own ranches. Alec Connell, who had recently bought the Gallup ranch (where the Dells had seen the last buffalo hide) owned the third. Lizzie sometimes felt like a mother to these single men, even though she was younger than them.

The neighbors were thankful that a woman—especially one who turned out to be such a good cook—had settled relatively close by. They were frequently invited by the Dells to join them for a meal, and they usually pitched in to help with some of the cooking or dishwashing.

At about this time, Sitting Bull—already famous for being the Indian who most White people believed had killed the great General Custer—was about to begin his rise to true celebrity status.

Alvaren Allen, the owner of the Merchant's Hotel where Sitting Bull and his group had stayed that spring in St. Paul, Minnesota, was also a showman. Allen had heard Sitting Bull give his railroad speech, and he thought the chief could make him a lot of money with similar performances in the future.

Allen wrote to Agent McLaughlin to ask his permission for Sitting Bull to go on tour with Allen's show. McLaughlin did not mind letting Sitting Bull leave the reservation; he figured it was better if the chief wasn't around to stir up trouble. McLaughlin happily agreed to Allen's request.

The show would be called The Sitting Bull Connection and several Indians from Sitting Bull's Lakota would also perform in it. Any profits from the show would be used to build school houses for Indian children, after the performers were paid and Allen took his share of the money.

Annie Oakley

The Indians traveled by train to St. Paul, Minnesota, where they spent a week getting their show costumes fitted.

In St. Paul, Sitting Bull met Annie Oakley for the first time. The young woman, famous for her sharpshooting abilities, was performing in a show at the Olympic Theater called Wild West. Colonel William "Buffalo Bill" Cody had put that show together the previous year.

Sitting Bull could not believe that Annie could perform such amazing feats with her rifle. He thought she must have supernatural powers.

She could shoot a dime right out of her husband's hand. When an assistant dropped a five of spades playing card from the top of a flagpole, Annie could quickly shoot the center spade out of the card as it fell! She could even accurately shoot a target behind her by looking at the reflection of it in the blade of a hunting knife.

After watching her impressive act, Sitting Bull asked if he could go backstage to meet her. The two hit it off immediately, and Sitting Bull later claimed to have "adopted" her. He had recently lost a daughter about Annie's age, so that might have been one reason for their quick friendship.

Annie Oakley thought Sitting Bull was a wonderful man who treated her like a "little pet." He fondly called her "Wantanya Cicilia," which someone loosely translated to "Little Sure Shot." After that, Annie used the "Little Sure Shot" nickname throughout her entire career.

As soon as the Indians' costumes were finished in St. Paul, Sitting Bull and his group left by train for New York City to perform in Allen's Indian show.

They stayed at New York's fancy Grand Central Hotel. Most of the White people who saw them had never seen Indians before, so the Indians were quite a novelty.

And the Indians were not familiar with some of the polite habits of most city people. For example, one Indian did not know what to do with his cloth napkin before dinner. He carefully unfolded it, looked at it, and finally decided to drape it across the seat of his chair. Then, he sat on it.

That same night, the Indians gathered in one of their rooms to hold a sacred pipe ceremony. However, when heavy smoke began to billow from the guest room, the hotel management had to ask them to stop because of complaints from other hotel guests.

If Sitting Bull had been impressed by St. Paul, Minnesota, he was amazed by New York City! There were huge crowds of people, buildings taller than he knew existed, and giant ships docked at the piers.

However, when reporters asked him what surprised him the most about the great city, Sitting Bull's reply was not what they expected. He said he was saddened to see so many White children begging for money on the streets when they instead ought to be at play like Indian children. While most Indian children were also poor, their families looked after them and would never allow them to beg from strangers.

In September, The Sitting Bull Connection tour finally began.

In October, a Sioux Indian named Luther Standing Bear saw the show when it was performed in Philadelphia, Pennsylvania. And he was surprised by what he saw and heard.

Sitting Bull and four other Indian men sat on the stage along with two women and two children. A White man came on stage and introduced Sitting Bull as the Indian who had killed the great General Custer, which of course was not true.

Sitting Bull then stood and addressed the audience in the Lakota language. He said, "My friends, White people, we Indians are on our way to Washington, D.C., to see the Grandfather (President of the United States). I see so many White people and what they are doing, that it makes me glad to know that someday my children will be educated also."

"There is no use fighting any longer. The buffalo are gone, as well as the rest of the [wild] game. Now I am going to shake

44

the hand of the Grandfather in Washington, and I am going to tell him all these things." He then sat without ever mentioning Custer's name.

The White interpreter then stood and pretended to translate Sitting Bull's Lakota into English. Luther Standing Bear spoke both Lakota and English so he listened carefully.

The interpreter failed to translate what Sitting Bull actually said. Instead he told the audience about the Battle of the Little Big Horn. He incorrectly explained how Sitting Bull and his warriors had quickly overpowered and then killed Custer and his soldiers. Luther Standing Bear couldn't believe all the lies the White interpreter told. But the audience seemed completely captivated.

It isn't known if Luther Standing Bear reported his findings back to Sitting Bull, but apparently no corrections were made to the rest of the shows. So, the lie about Sitting Bull and Custer continued to be spread.

After their final show, the Indians headed back west by train to the reservations. At the St. Paul station stop, a reporter climbed on board their train car to interview Sitting Bull about the trip. The chief told him he especially liked the dancing girls he had seen in New York City. Sitting Bull stood and demonstrated their wiggly dance movements, causing everyone in the train car to burst into laughter.

Back in the Cave Hills, Lizzie and George were looking forward to the birth of their first child.

In late October, they drove the **buckboard** wagon 100 miles north to the nearest train line at the town of Dickinson. There, Lizzie planned to take the train by herself back to Cresco, Iowa. She wanted to stay at her parents' farm so a doctor would be close by when needed at the time of her child's birth.

Buckboard Road to Dickinson

Dickinson Train Depot 1909

The buckboard ride took three days. The couple slept overnight in the back of the wagon with a pile of blankets and quilts to keep them warm. After arriving in Dickinson, George said goodbye to Lizzie at the train station, and then headed back to the ranch where there was plenty of work awaiting him.

On Thanksgiving Day, November 27, 1884, Lizzie gave birth to a baby girl much earlier than she had expected. The baby was born before the doctor, who was twenty miles away that day, could be fetched. Female family and friends helped Lizzie during the childbirth. She and George had already decided to name the baby (if it was a girl) Mathilde [ma-til-da] after Lizzie's mother, Mathilde Malek Halweg.

The tiny baby was placed in a wooden box that they put behind the stove in the kitchen, the warmest place in the house. Mathilde, nicknamed Tillie, was an especially quiet baby who slept for eight or nine hours at a time and did not open her eyes for almost an entire month. Whenever she was awake, they fed her a teaspoon or two of milk mixed with a little water.

When Lizzie told the doctor that she was concerned about Tillie's closed eyes and lack of crying, the doctor told her not to worry. He smiled and said, "You will know soon enough that there is a new baby in the house."

George did not learn for several months that the couple's new baby was a girl, because the mail traveled so slowly.

Back in the Dakota Territory, George continued with the daily duties at the Triple-C Ranch. He and his men were also working hard on a big surprise for Lizzie's return, which he knew would help her feel more settled.

## THE MAIL

In the early years, all of the mail for the Cave Hills ranchers was delivered to Camp Crook, a small town about thirty miles to the west. When the cowboys needed to go into town, they brought back the mail and left it all at the Dell ranch. The delivering cowboy, on his own horse, led a pony with two sacks of mail strapped on it. The mail usually came to the Dells' three-to-six months after its arrival in Camp Crook.

Once, Lizzie received a letter from a relative in New Jersey. The cowboy who was bringing it from Camp Crook to the Dells was supposedly shot and killed in a saloon brawl. When emptying his pockets, some other cowboys who were with him took the letter with the intent to deliver it to Lizzie. When she finally received the letter, it was covered with dried blood. The cowboys claimed this was because they had butchered a cow on their way to her. She wasn't sure what to believe about the source of the blood.

For Lizzie, one of the most important items to arrive in the mail every year was a new calendar sent from her mother in Cresco. Lizzie liked to keep track of the days and weeks. She was a deeply religious person and wanted to observe every Sunday in addition to reading her German Bible every day. Lizzie said, "I think that everyone who lives in a wilderness needs their Bible to read and to keep near to God."

The neighbor men used to say Lizzie didn't need a calendar to know when Sunday was. They joked that anyone could tell it was Sunday when Dells' cowboys had clean shirts on.

The long delay in getting the news many times left the Dells unaware of what was going on in the country. United States' President Ulysses Grant was dead for three months before they heard about it. One day a cowboy rode up to the ranch and told them the news. He handed George a newspaper account of it to read, and then he asked for the newspaper back so he could take it to the next ranch.

# CHAPTER FOUR – THE WILD WEST (1885)

In the spring of 1885, Lizzie returned by train to the Dakota Territory. But she traveled to Dickinson alone. She felt that Tillie's delicate health was not well-suited for the daily hardships of prairie life, so she left the baby in her grandparents' care on the farm in Iowa.

Americans at that time (including Lizzie and George) considered the Dakota Territory part of the "Wild West." It had none of the modern conveniences such as good roads, fences, access to medical care, or even laws to follow.

Conditions in the Dakotas were challenging even for the strongest, healthiest people. The weather extremes were highly unpredictable. One day it could be 45 degrees above zero and the next day 40 degrees below. The winters brought howling winds with bitter cold. Blizzards often buried and froze people and ranch animals.

The summers were often unbearably hot and prairie fires were a constant threat. Black mosquitos were terrible pests, so bad in the early summer that people had to cover their faces with a scarf or handkerchief in order to breathe. The mosquitos could cover a horse so completely that a person could no longer tell its color.

Cougars, wolves, and rattlesnakes could be dangerous predators. Cattle were particularly vulnerable to attacks from them. In the fall of each year, the ranchers poured poison on chunks of raw meat and left them outside to kill the wolves. Once, George even had to shoot a wolf that came too close to the Dells' cabin.

George picked up Lizzie at the train station in Dickinson, and together they made the trip back to their ranch on Bull Creek. As they approached their homestead, Lizzie was delighted to discover George's surprise for her. He and his cowboys had built a much larger home during the winter. The house had a stone foundation and the wood walls were made from cottonwood logs. It had a combined sitting room and kitchen in the center, and two bedrooms, one at either end. Everyone would now have a real bed and would no longer have to sleep on skinny raised wooden-plank beds or on the floor. Lizzie clapped her hands in delight as George proudly walked her through their new home.

There was also a separate wooden bunkhouse for the cowboys, outbuildings for food storage and meat smoking, and corrals for the cattle and horses.

George thought it would save Lizzie floor-scrubbing time to have a simple dirt floor like they had in their first house. But

The Dell Cabin circa 1930

because there were so many more rooms to move around in, Lizzie found the bottom of her skirts often became filthy by noontime. Soon, more lumber was ordered and the men laid a wood floor.

Lizzie made window curtains out of some old dress fabric and trimmed them with lace from an old shawl. The beds were covered with cozy and colorful handmade quilts she had brought from Iowa. She decorated the house with bowls of fragrant yellow clover blossoms, sprigs of sage, and pinecones.

The Dells' newest neighbor, whom they called "Virginia Bill" Hamilton (because he originally came from Virginia), later said the couple had "the best house in the Hills."

Once back in the Dakota Territory, Lizzie kept busy in her new, larger home. In addition to cleaning house and doing laundry, she spent a great deal of time cooking and baking. She was glad to have their cowboys and the Dells' male neighbors around to appreciate her cooking skills!

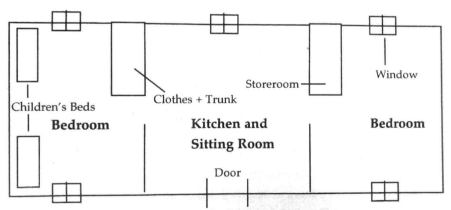

Diagram of the second Dell cabin, 1885

Some of Lizzie's typical meals, often served with coffee, included:

Breakfast
- Bacon
- Fried eggs (when the hens cooperated by laying some)
- Baking powder biscuits or bread

Lunch (their main meal)
- Beef, deer, antelope meat, or bacon
- Canned tomatoes, peaches, and apricots

Dinner
- Potatoes (Lizzie had a small patch growing near the cabin)
- Canned fruit
- Dessert of cake, pie, or sugar cookies (Lizzie's father had owned a large bakery in Germany when she was little, so he had taught her to make delicious baked goods)

Lizzie and George often watched for grazing deer and antelope through a **field glass** they owned. If they spotted one, George would shoot it so they had more meat to eat.

The cowboys had never eaten mincemeat, so when Lizzie made a mincemeat pie, they thought it was a real treat! Because of the poor soil in that area, Lizzie did not have a vegetable garden (except for her potato patch), but she did have access to the many wild fruits that grew in the area, so she made jams and jellies using wild berries and plums.

The cowboys loved Lizzie's baked doughnuts!

In the evenings after Lizzie fed her family and the cowboys, and all of them helped her clean up, they would settle into their typical nighttime routine. George and the other men played cards at the table, while Lizzie sat in her rocker and read or sewed. A kerosene lantern and candles gave the room a warm glow and provided all the light they needed.

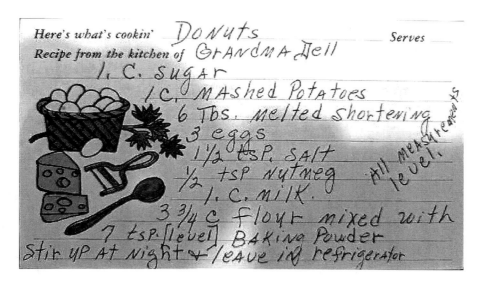

Here's what's cookin' Donuts   Serves ___
Recipe from the kitchen of Grandma Dell
1 C. sugar
1 C. mashed potatoes
6 Tbs. melted shortening
3 eggs
1½ tsp. salt
½ tsp nutmeg
1 C. milk
3¾ C flour mixed with
7 tsp. [level] baking powder
Stir up at night & leave in refrigerator

All measurements level

The winter of 1885-1886 was Lizzie's first winter in the Dakotas. It was brutally cold, with howling winds and temperatures dropping as low as forty-five degrees below zero. She and her little family of cowboys spent a great deal of time indoors near the woodstove trying to keep warm.

Even though George was just forty years old when he and Lizzie arrived in the Dakota Territory, the neighbors all called him "Old Man Dell." He had a somewhat stern look at times, but according to their neighbor, "Virginia Bill" Hamilton, he was quite a prankster.

According to a tale told by "Virginia Bill," their neighbor Alec Connell came to Old Man Dell and asked him how to kill a skunk without causing a bad odor. Alec had cut a cat hole into the door of his log house so his cat could come and go as it pleased. But late every night a skunk would come through the cat hole into the house and Alec wanted to get rid of the skunk once and for all.

George told Alec the easiest way to kill a skunk was to hard boil an egg, cut it open, mix the yolk with poison, and put the egg back together. Then, lay it on the floor so the skunk would eat it and that would kill him.

Alec thanked George for his advice and decided to give it a try. After dark that night, Alec set up a small kerosene lamp near the cat hole and he and his cowboys watched from their beds. Sure enough, pretty soon the skunk crawled in through the cat hole, ate the egg, and began convulsing from the poison. Unfortunately, he proceeded to spray his stinky musk all over inside the house before he died. Alec and his cowboys grabbed their bedding and ran outside as fast as they could to get away from the stench. It took weeks of repeatedly scrubbing the floor with **lye** to get the smell out. They had to sleep outside all summer, rain or shine.

It appeared as though "Old Man Dell" had pulled a fast one on Alec. The next time Alec Connell saw George Dell, he asked him if he hadn't known better about the effect of killing a skunk that way. George just chuckled and said yes, he did know better.

That spring, Sitting Bull was invited to join Buffalo Bill Cody's Wild West show—the same show at which Sitting Bull had met Annie Oakley the previous year. Buffalo Bill had attended one of the shows of The Sitting Bull Connection tour and had been impressed by what a sensation the chief had been.

Buffalo Bill thought that people in large cities would pay to see real cowboys and Indians up close. He was right. In 1882, when he opened his first Buffalo Bill Cody's Wild West show, people turned out by the thousands—up to 20,000 per show!

Buffalo Bill sought to make his show as realistic as possible, since he knew that the real wild west was quickly disappearing. In the first couple of years, he added a real stagecoach from the town of Deadwood, and live bears and buffalo. In 1885, he

Buffalo Bill's Wild West Show Opening

Sitting Bull and Buffalo Bill Cody

was pleased to add a famous Indian to the show, Chief Sitting Bull. Sitting Bull was delighted when he learned that his new friend and "adopted daughter," Annie Oakley—Little Sure Shot—would star in the show with him, so he quickly accepted Buffalo Bill's offer.

In 1885, Sitting Bull and Buffalo Bill were pictured together shaking hands on a poster advertising the show.

The show featured Sitting Bull for four months and he quickly became its biggest star. He was paid $50 a week plus an extra $125 bonus if he stayed in the show for the full four months.

People continued to flock to the show. They wanted to see for themselves this Indian who they heard had completely wiped out General Custer and his troops in what would become the most famous war between Indians and White people in US history.

The chief's role in the show was easy; all he had to do was dress the part. Every time he went on stage, he wore his **war bonnet**. To Buffalo Bill's credit, Sitting Bull was never advertised as "the Indian who killed General Custer." Buffalo Bill knew better than to lie to the public, for fear of hurting his own reputation. (But he certainly didn't hesitate to exaggerate!) It didn't matter though—the crowds still believed Sitting Bull was personally responsible for Custer's death, so they usually booed when he came on stage.

However, when the show went to Canada the crowds there did not boo Sitting Bull. Many cheered for the chief because they understood the Sioux had been treated unfairly by the US government.

Sitting Bull did not take part in the show's staged battles and its **tableaus** [tah blōs] with the other cowboys and Indians. He did, however, ride his horse in the show's ceremonial parades, wearing his war bonnet and carrying a feather-decorated **lance**, club, and shield. After his act, he climbed into the stands to sit

Sitting Bull in War Bonnet

and watch the rest of the show. He tapped his feet to the music and always seemed to enjoy watching the action.

Upon Sitting Bull's request, Buffalo Bill had provided tipis for the Lakota to stay in during the show so they would feel more at home than in a city hotel. Also, their lodgings would seem more authentic to the visitors who toured the show grounds.

After the show, Sitting Bull greeted visitors and reporters at his tipi. Sitting Bull found it curious how the same people who had booed him during the show always lined up to get his autograph afterwards.

Annie Oakley later said Sitting Bull was like an "open-handed uncle" to all the newspaper boys and shoeshine boys they met on the tour. He never bought a newspaper from them, because he reportedly could not read English. And he did not need his beaded, suede moccasins shined by them either. But he always had silver coins to pass out to the boys.

The show's grand **finale** [fi nal ee] always included a light gray horse of Buffalo Bill's standing on its hind legs. It would rear up at the sound of gunshots, and wave its front hooves in the air. When the tour ended, Buffalo Bill gave the horse, named Rico, to Sitting Bull as a gift and even paid for its transportation by train to the Dakotas.

Sitting Bull was relieved when Buffalo Bill's Wild West show ended. He had grown tired of the hustle and bustle of big city life and was ready to get back to the fresh air and slower pace of the real wild west.

Horse "Rico"

# CHAPTER FIVE –
# THE VISITOR (1886)

Sitting Bull was a medicine man, but he was nothing like our modern-day doctors. For the Indians, a medicine man was a spiritual leader for the nation, a person who prayed to the spirits through ceremonies and rituals for a vision (imaginations while awake) he might use to help his followers.

The Lakota believed that everything—the buffalo, the eagle, the sun, the earth, the sky, the wind—had a spirit which was connected to Wakan Tanka, the Great Spirit and Creator. Sitting Bull felt Wakan Tanka had chosen him to use his gifts to help his people, the Lakota Sioux.

It has been said that Sitting Bull could interpret his dreams and had mystical visions which he often shared with his people. They believed he had special powers and could even control the weather and the animals that lived around them. When the Lakota faced bad luck, they would look to their spiritual leader, Sitting Bull, for guidance.

One vision, in particular, clearly foretold of Custer's defeat in 1876. In another vision in August of 1890 (just months before his own death), Sitting Bull saw a meadowlark alight on a little hill beside him, and heard it say, "One of your own people, a Lakota, will kill you." That vision also later came true.

The Lakota often traveled in covered wagons through the Dakota Territory. Indians on horseback also pulled **travois** [tra voy] behind them, which carried the supplies needed to quickly put up their tipis when they stopped.

Cheyenne Indians using a travois, 1890

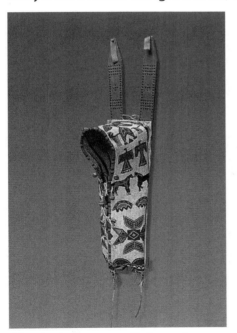

Above: Lakota cradleboard
Right: Woman from Ute tribe with a baby in cradleboard, 1899

The Sioux women rode astride like men, with one leg on each side of the saddle. Their babies and toddlers were tightly laced into their **cradleboards**, which were often attached to a travois or to a horse.

Barking, flea-bitten dogs often accompanied the group. If wild game could not be found, sometimes one of the dogs would be killed and cooked over the fire for dinner.

When possible, the Sioux shortened travel time by traveling in a straight line "as the crow flies." Instead of moving alongside a shallow, winding creek, they crossed it each time the creek wound its way into their path. The Sioux called this practice "threading the needle."

The Lakota often stopped along the way to find water, hunt, eat, sleep, and rest their horses. They set up their tipis like we would put up a group of tents today at a campsite. Within the tipis each person had their own place where they sat during the day and also slept at night.

The Indian women were modest and did not undress at night. They simply loosened their clothing, took off their shoes, and let down their hair. Even so, the Indian men waited outdoors until the women went to bed. Then the men quietly entered the tipi and went to their own places to sleep. In the morning, the men disappeared until the women had prepared for their day.

The Lakota men and women had highly defined roles each of which was considered equally important.

The Indian women were in charge of setting up and later tearing down the camp. They unpacked the wagons and put the tipis together. When it was time to move again, they took the tipis down and repacked the wagons.

The women prepared animal hides for clothing and warm bedding. They sewed the hides for clothing and for the tipis,

Sioux Camp

Lakota Moccasins

and also made moccasins and boots from the hides. They dyed cut-up porcupine quills with brilliant colors and sewed them onto the footwear using their own unique geometric designs for decorations. Sometimes they used colorful glass beads from the trading posts for the same purpose. The women also made extra moccasins that they sold to White people for $1 a pair.

The women also crafted utensils and food containers from animal bones and hooves. They cut meat, dried it when necessary (so it would keep longer), and cooked all of the meals. The women were in charge of the home, and they were devoted to their families.

The men hunted and took care of the horses. They crafted hunting arrows and hatchets, cleaned and mended weapons, and repaired wagons and travois. The men were the providers of food and protectors of the tribe, and they also helped look after the children.

In the spring of 1886, Lizzie Dell returned to Iowa from the Dakotas to give birth to another baby at her parents' farm. She was also happy to spend the summer in Iowa with her daughter, Tillie, whom she had not seen for over a year. On the morning of August 8th, her family (her parents, her brother Charles, and Tillie) woke up and dressed for a neighborhood wedding. Lizzie stayed home to rest, since her baby was due to be born soon.

Shortly after her family had left the house, Lizzie's labor pains began. Since there was no one to fetch the doctor and there were no telephones, Lizzie had to deliver the baby by herself. Later that day, when her family returned from the wedding, they were very surprised to meet Lizzie's first son, John.

In the summer of 1886, while Lizzie was back in Iowa, Sitting Bull and some of his followers were crossing the prairie near the Dells' land. Possibly they were returning home from the site of the Battle of the Little Bighorn. On June 25th there had been a 10-year commemoration of the battle there, where many Sioux had danced and celebrated their famous victory over General Custer and his cavalry.

One day, while his people set up camp, Sitting Bull rode away with four Indian men including an interpreter. His eyes were badly infected and he was in a great deal of pain, possibly the result of his participation in the Sun Dance. Sitting Bull needed to find someone who could help him relieve the terrible soreness in his eyes.

Eventually, Sitting Bull's group came across Bull Creek and followed it until they came upon a long log cabin. George and his men were outdoors when they saw the approaching Indians. The Indians brought their horses to a slow walk so as not to frighten the White men. George could tell these were reservation Indians, as they were mostly dressed in White men's clothing. Even so, it was fortunate that Lizzie had not yet returned from Iowa. She later said she would have hidden under a bed in fear had she been there!

The Indians raised the index and middle fingers of their right hands like a closed peace sign, which George knew meant hello in their own sign language.

Sitting Bull's interpreter explained they were from the Lakota nation at Standing Rock Reservation to the east and had come in peace. He went on to explain why they were there. Sitting Bull was desperate for White man's medicine for his eyes. He was in terrible pain and needed help.

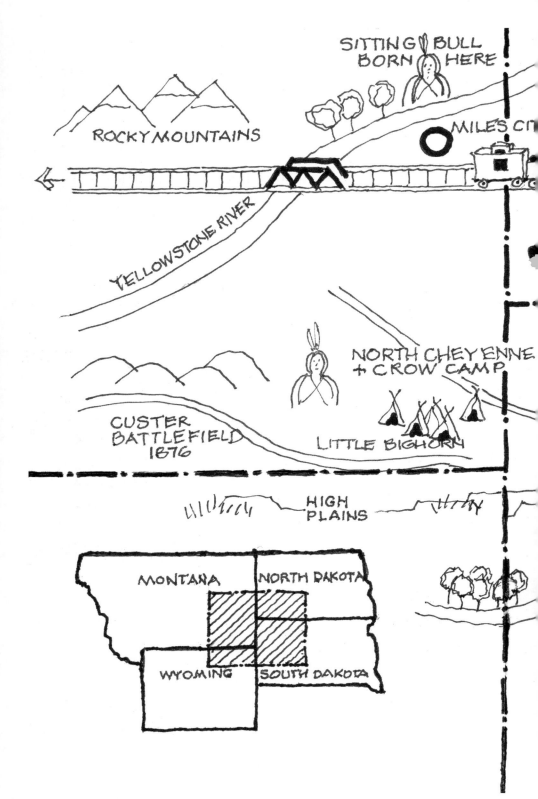

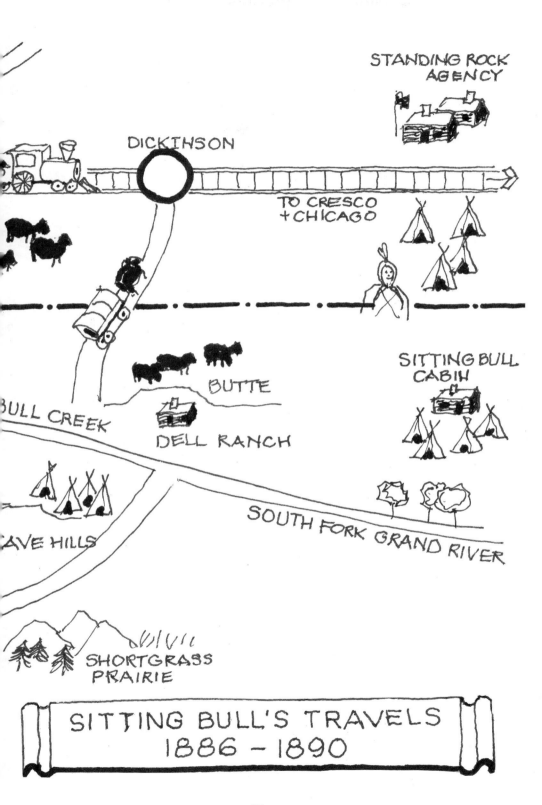

## THE SUN DANCE

Wiwang Wacipi ("Gazing at the Sun While You Dance"), shortened to the "Sun Dance" by white culture, is a Sioux ceremony performed by individuals for the continued health and life of the entire Sioux nation.

Men danced for four days without food or water, and showed how much pain they could tolerate by staring at the sun for long periods of time without flinching. A man was expected to give all his energy to this dance. In this ritual, the Indians offered prayers to the Great Spirit Wakan Tanka. Wakan Tanka was part of every living thing—people, animals, trees, and plants.

Sitting Bull wanted to be known as a Sun Dancer.

George invited the Indians to dismount and come inside the cabin, while his cowboys helped tie up their horses to the corral fence.

George's experience as a medic in the Civil War had provided him with some knowledge about curing ailments. He also consulted the medicine book he had brought from Iowa, for information about how to make an ointment for Sitting Bull's eyes. George gave him some extra medicine, as well, so Sitting Bull could continue the treatment on his own. The chief seemed grateful.

George offered to feed the group, since he had bacon, potatoes, and canned goods on hand. The Indians accepted the invitation, and all the men ate a meal together.

Afterward, Sitting Bull asked if George and his men would like to smoke a sacred pipe with the Indians. They nodded yes.

Sitting Bull pulled out his sacred pipe, pressed some tobacco into it, and lit it with a match. He then puffed out three clouds of smoke and passed the pipe to the next man in the group.

The interpreter explained that each of the men should take one puff and then pass the pipe to the next man. Each man took a puff until the pipe made its way back to Sitting Bull. Then, the chief blew smoke to the four winds (the four directions) before ending the ceremony and tapping out the ashes.

Although a typical Indian man's most prized possession was perhaps his warhorse, his pipe may have come in a close second. Pipes were prized because their bowls were beautifully-carved pieces of art and the pipes also represented a very sacred ceremony to the Indians.

The pipe-smoking ritual was rarely done solely for pleasure, but instead signified special occasions, like welcoming a guest or sealing a new friendship. The Indians believed the pipe was sacred, and that all people who smoked it together pledged to live peacefully.

Never having smoked an Indian pipe before, George appreciated the beauty of the pipe and was pleased the Indians had shared this special tradition with him. George asked the interpreter to share his feelings with Sitting Bull, and the chief beamed despite his eye pain.

George asked if he could buy the pipe as a souvenir of Sitting Bull's visit. He wanted to show it to Lizzie and tell her all about the event when she returned from Iowa.

Sitting Bull said he would sell George the pipe for $5 (the equivalent of about $125 today) on one condition: Whenever Sitting Bull came back for a visit they would always smoke the pipe together to celebrate their friendship.

The Indians then returned to the reservation, where Agent McLaughlin continued to look for opportunities to safely send Sitting Bull away from there. He thought there seemed to be less trouble when the chief wasn't around.

## THE SACRED PIPE

Various types of ceremonial pipes were and still are made by American Indians. The Lakota sacred pipe is called a cannupa in the Lakota language.

The Lakota sacred pipes have long, wooden stems, with pipe bowls made from catlinite, which is also called pipestone. Pipestone is a somewhat soft clay stone which is found between layers of a much harder stone called Sioux quartzite. Only Native American Indians are allowed to **quarry** the stone at the Pipestone National Monument, which is located near the town of Pipestone in south-western Minnesota.

The pipe that Sitting Bull sold to George Dell had a common T-shaped design. However, the unique pipe-bowl piece featured raised circular ridges with a recessed space between them, which is a difficult carving technique. It is not known who made the pipe. The very personal pipe was used in sending prayers to God, confirming peace, sealing a new agreement, or cementing a friendship.

One day, a letter arrived inviting Sitting Bull and his followers to visit the Crow Indians in Montana. The Crow had recently sold over thirty million acres of their former lands to the US Government and were now living on a reservation.

The Crow had been fierce enemies of the Sioux in the past. Sitting Bull's own father had been killed by a Crow. But since the 1860s some of the Sioux and Crow thought they should work to become allies to strengthen their defense against the White people. The Crow even promised gifts of ponies to their Lakota visitors.

East of the Crow's Indian agency in Montana was the Tongue River Reservation, home of the Northern Cheyenne Indians. The Northern Cheyenne were friends and allies of the Lakota, and Sitting Bull hoped to see them, too, on the trip.

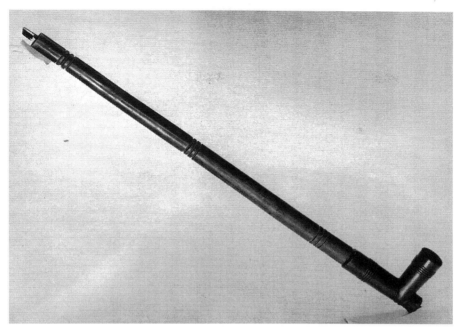

Pipe sold to George Dell by Sitting Bull

In September 1886, over 100 Sioux from the Standing Rock and Cheyenne River Reservations asked Indian officials for permission to visit the Crow Reservation. Permission was granted, and Sitting Bull and his followers soon took off for Montana Territory.

When they had the opportunity to visit far-flung relatives and friends, the Indians always went with great enthusiasm. Agent McLaughlin later reported that "there never were people like my red friends to go visiting." Perhaps they found such trips to be comforting as they allowed the Indians to behave as they used to. This time, the promise of free ponies also sweetened the trip!

For two weeks, the Crow and their guests shared memories, feasted, and smoked their pipes in friendship.

In late September 1886, George took the train alone to Cresco, Iowa. After a few days at Lizzie's parents' farm, he and Lizzie traveled back to the Dakota Territory on the train carrying their new baby John in a large shoe box. Again, the couple decided to leave Tillie behind in Cresco with her grandparents. The little girl, a toddler not yet two years old, had grown very close to Lizzie's parents, so Lizzie and George did not want to tear her away from them.

At their destination, Dickinson, they bought provisions to last the next few months on their ranch. And by early October, they headed towards home. It had snowed early that year, and the ground was already covered with six inches of snow as they traveled. George drove the wagon with a pair of horses while Lizzie lay in the back on a featherbed, napping and nursing their two-month-old baby. The first night of their short trip they slept in the wagon, covered up with all the blankets they had. But they were still so cold that Lizzie and George were very worried about their baby John.

The next night, they longed for a warmer place to stay, so they traveled a little out of their way to a ranch with a store called Buckskin Joe's. Buckskin Joe made and sold buckskin

BURY THE HATCHET
The phrase, "bury the hatchet," when used today, means to settle your differences with someone. But some American Indian nations actually buried a hatchet or axe under the ground, from each enemy tribe, when they decided to make peace. Other American Indians sometimes used the phrase as we do today, without actually burying any tools.

jackets and gloves for boys, and he lived in a ranch house with the George Mattock family. Mrs. Mattock was known to keep the house nice and warm in the wintertime, and she welcomed the Dells with comfortable beds to sleep on. Before they went to bed, Mrs. Mattock gave little John some warm catnip tea and helped Lizzie bundle him up in blankets that had been warmed by the fire.

The next afternoon, the Dells arrived back home at the Triple-C Ranch. The cowboys had been expecting them for several days and already had a nice fire going in their fireplace.

Dickinson, 1882

For the next few days, baby John had trouble getting to sleep, and his lack of sleep made him cranky. Sleep had been no problem for him when he was being jolted on the trip home in their buckboard wagon across the hard, snow-covered dirt roads. So, George used an axe to build the baby a rough cradle from a wooden grocery box. The plunk-plunk sound it made as it rocked was like music to the baby's ears and he fell asleep right away!

It seemed that every time Lizzie returned from Iowa, George had a surprise for her or a story to tell about something that had happened while she was away. Last year the surprise was their new house!

This time, he told her about his visitor, Chief Sitting Bull, and he showed her the pipe as he related the story about it. Lizzie was excited to hear about the Indians' visit to the ranch. She had read in the newspapers about Sitting Bull's appearance in Buffalo Bill's Wild West Show and she knew that he was a famous Indian chief who lived at Standing Rock Reservation. His visit to their ranch would be like a famous sports or music celebrity visiting someone's house today.

But the first time Sitting Bull came to the Dell ranch when Lizzie was home, she was a bit wary. However, he quickly won her over with a broad smile that lit up his entire face. He and some of his Lakota followers brought many gifts for the Dells, as well. They presented Lizzie and little John with handmade, beaded moccasins. They also brought beaver, antelope, and deer hides for the family, which Lizzie and George gratefully accepted. These would soon come into good use as warm rugs and bed throws in the house as well as cozy bedding for their buckboard wagon.

Sitting Bull stood nearly six feet tall, and the Dells' neighbor, "Virginia Bill," said the chief had the broadest shoulders he had ever seen. Sitting Bull's face was **pockmarked** from smallpox that he had caught early in his life, and he walked with a limp, having been shot in the foot, in his early 20's, by a Crow Indian warrior (whom he then killed). He wore his straight, dark hair braided to his waist in Lakota fashion. Aside from his beaded moccasins, he was dressed like a White man in a long-sleeved **calico** shirt and a pair of trousers. He wore a black hat with a brim and a red scarf knotted around his neck.

Lizzie was twenty-three years old, and Sitting Bull, who was around fifty-five at the time, was soon treating her almost like a daughter. His interest in the White man's ways certainly extended to the Dells. He was curious about Lizzie's daily chores, whether she was sewing on a button or baking a pie. He was also curious what George and his men were doing, especially if it involved the day-to-day operations of the cattle ranch. Sitting Bull had a natural curiosity and loved learning about everything.

The chief was also charismatic. His notable biographer, Robert M. Utley, wrote that Sitting Bull had a "forceful personality, superior intellect, and personal magnetism."

Lizzie told family members back in Iowa he was the most intelligent man she had ever known in her life. Sitting Bull had likely impressed the Dells with his knowledge of nature, including healing plants and herbs, animal behavior, and weather patterns.

Sitting Bull and his Indians came to George and Lizzie's ranch at least every spring and fall when they left the reservation to hunt deer and antelope. They always camped on Bull Creek in front of the Dells' cabin. The creek served as a low place that was good for protection from wind and cold. The Indians would set up their cone-shaped, animal-hide tipis and place buffalo hides on the ground inside for comfortable sitting and sleeping. In warm weather, the Indians built cooking fires outside. In cold weather, they built fires for cooking and warmth in the middle of the tipis' dirt floors with the smoke exiting from openings at the tipis' tops.

Despite the reputation of the Sioux as being somewhat standoffish around White people, the Dells found Sitting Bull and his followers to be friendly and sociable once both groups of people became comfortable with each other's company. Lizzie and George enjoyed their visits and began to look forward to them.

The Lakota women were especially talkative. Much like many White women, they gossiped with one another, laughed and chatted freely with their relatives, and teased and scolded their husbands. The women were also curious about Lizzie, since they saw few White women on or near the reservation. They seemed to enjoy Lizzie's visits to their camp along Bull Creek, and always treated her as an honored guest.

Many homesteaders held negative opinions about the Indians, most likely from accounts, true or false, that they'd heard, so they did not trust the Indians. But the Dell family was an exception. As their granddaughter Jean Bieler Hastings wrote many decades later, "They developed a friendly relationship with the Sioux leader,"—an attitude they held for the rest of their lives. To their credit, George and Lizzie's cowboys and neighbors also grew comfortable with Sitting Bull and his followers.

Sitting Bull sometimes visited the Dell ranch alone without any of his tribe with him.

Once, when Sitting Bull came by himself, he asked by sign language how Lizzie and George were doing. All he had to do was raise his eyebrows and point at them and they understood what he was asking.

Many Indians used a type of sign language to communicate with other Indian nations. The hand signs they made were basic and were used along with facial expressions.

A cupped hand gestured toward the mouth with the palm facing down and finger tips touching meant hunger or food, while a cupped hand held below the mouth with the palm up meant thirst or drink. A hand sweeping out to the right from the heart meant "good," while throwing a pretend item down on the ground meant "bad."

When Sitting Bull asked by sign language how the Dells were doing, George indicated, with a grimace on his face and a finger pointing at one ear, that he was in pain from a bad earache.

By pretending to smoke, Sitting Bull motioned to George to get out the pipe. Sitting Bull took some tobacco out of a little pouch, filled the pipe, and then lit it.

He motioned to George to come closer to him, took a long puff on the pipe, and then blew the smoke toward George's sore ear. He did this several times until the pipe was finished. Later, George swore that his earache had then gone away.

# CHAPTER SIX - YOUR FRIENDS ARE COMING! (1887)

The winter of 1886-1887 was even worse than the previous winter. Blizzards began in November, creating snow drifts up to seven feet high. At first, the snow was soft and the cows could paw through it to find food. But a warm, rainy spell in December caused the top to melt and then later freeze into a thick, solid layer of ice when the cold returned. The cows could not break through the ice to get to their food.

Some cows died of starvation, while others fell through the high, iced-over snow drifts and suffocated in the soft snow below. Temperatures dropped down to 40 below zero with dangerous winds, and people stayed indoors whenever possible. Even if the ranchers could have found the scattered cattle on the plains, there was nothing they could do for them, and they would have put their own lives at great risk searching for the animals.

The snow continued falling in the new year, and by January it was at least three-to-four feet deep on the prairie, with drifts taller than humans and even some buildings.

In March, when the snow finally melted, thousands of dead cattle lay everywhere. By late spring the odor of rotting carcasses was so bad that the homesteaders could not leave a door or window open in their houses.

The Dells and their neighbors lost most of their cattle that winter. Some ranchers turned to raising horses or gave up on ranching altogether. George decided he would go back to Cresco in the fall, buy more cattle, and start over.

In April of 1887, the Dells traveled to Dickinson to buy provisions again. George made this trip, usually with Lizzie or one of the cowboys, three times a year, in April, July, and September.

A typical load of provisions for the ranch included:

- A few 48-pound fabric sacks of flour (the sacks were made of white cotton and would later be cut up to make kitchen towels)
- 100-pound sacks of smoked breakfast bacon
- Several 50-pound boxes of coffee
- A barrel (196 pounds) of sugar
- Lemons (these would keep for several weeks in water that was changed every few days)
- Raisins and currants
- Dried apples
- Cases of canned tomatoes and fruits (usually peaches or apricots)
- A dozen or so live chickens for eggs
- Grain for horse feed

In May, Lizzie and George took the buckboard to the Ox Ranch about forty miles away near the present town of Marmarth, North Dakota. The ranch was run by cowboys from Texas and the cook there, Louis Anderson, also served as cook on the roundups in which George's cowboys participated. There was a big wagon sale being held at the Ox Ranch and the Dells wanted to purchase a new wagon. They left home at three o'clock in the morning so they could get to the sale that same day before nightfall.

They arrived in time to purchase a new wagon, but it was too late in the day to leave for home, so they decided to spend the night. They were offered a room to sleep in so they would not have to sleep in the wagon. George and Lizzie were grateful for that offer of comfort, because they had nine-month-old John with them.

The next morning, one of the cowboys at the ranch roped a cow who had recently given birth to a new calf. Louis Anderson, the ranch cook, thought the mother cow could supply milk for the Dells' son, John. George, having been an Iowa farmer, was apparently the only man there who knew how to milk a cow so he immediately got to work. Anderson, however, teased the other men, because they all wanted fresh milk for their coffee, too. He pointed out that the ranch had thousands of cows and yet none of the men who worked there knew how to milk a cow. Now that morning they all wanted to take the baby's milk for their own coffee!

Heavy rains had caused dangerous flooding in that area, so the Dells had to stay at the Ox Ranch for several days. When they were finally able to leave, the cowboys let the cow and calf go free. The cook asked the ranch's cowboys why they didn't want to keep the cow for milk for their coffees, but not one of the men wanted to learn how to milk it. They even seemed insulted by the suggestion. Milking cows wasn't considered a real cowboy's work!

When the Dells reached the Little Missouri River, they found the water was still very high and too dangerous to cross by wagon. So, they turned around and drove their two wagons back to the Ox Ranch. When the cowboys saw them coming, they went back out to find the mother cow so George could milk her some more. The cowboys did not let the cow and her calf loose again until they were sure the Dells and their thirsty baby were gone for good. And everyone enjoyed fresh milk in their coffee while the Dells were there.

After the Dells returned home to the Triple-C Ranch, Sitting Bull came for a visit again. The Lakota came so frequently that George even kidded Lizzie about it. Whenever he saw the Indians approaching, he would holler, "Lizzie! Your friends are coming!"

She would often kid "Doctor Dell" in return, because sometimes the Indians came to ask George to dispense ointment for their eyes or **quinine** [kwi nine] for fevers. The Indians respected his knowledge of medicine, ever since he had successfully treated Sitting Bull's sore eyes on the chief's first visit to their cabin.

When the Lakota came to visit, they always brought animal skins and new moccasins for the family. When Lizzie discovered how comfortable the moccasins were, they became the only shoes she ever wore again at the ranch.

Lizzie loved to visit the Indians' camp, too. She found the women to be self-reliant and strong, but feminine in their mannerisms. They seemed curious about Lizzie and her lifestyle, and they laughed delightedly as they compared their clothing to hers. The only commonality was the colorful Indian moccasins they all wore.

Lizzie preferred simple, almost-floor-length dresses made of cotton or lightweight wool in darker colors that would stay clean-looking longer. Since she only had a few dresses she always wore an apron to protect them. In colder weather she added a shawl over her shoulders. The Lakota women giggled when Lizzie hiked up the bottom of her dress a bit to give them a peek at her white petticoat underneath.

The Indian women wore straight, calico dresses with wide, flowing sleeves. They belted their dresses with leather at the waist, and underneath they wore red or blue flannel leggings. A colorful shawl or blanket worn over the shoulders sometimes completed their outfits.

The women wore necklaces and bracelets of brass and shell. Some of the younger ones used red paint on their cheeks and along the part in the center of their dark, braided hair. The young, unmarried women acted with great modesty, lowering their heads and averting their eyes whenever men were present.

When the Indians visited the ranch, Sitting Bull, who by then spoke some English, would often take Lizzie to the storeroom, pat her on the shoulder and say, "I like you. I like you." Then he would point to items he wanted—usually coffee, sugar, and bacon.

Sitting Bull knew these would not be given to him for free. But Lizzie charged him much less than the agency charged. Sitting Bull told her the Indians paid $1 at the agency for the same amount of sugar that Lizzie sold him for 25 cents. She didn't lose money on the sale, since she paid only 4 1/2 cents for a pound of sugar in Dickinson. Lizzie did not feel guilty charging the Indians 25 cents for that sugar, because the trip back and forth to Dickinson took a week. The Dells and Sitting Bull both benefited from this arrangement. Lizzie and George often privately discussed how badly they thought the Indians were treated on the reservation and how little power they had to resist this injustice.

Lizzie fed the Indians every time they visited. George would say "Lizzie, don't you stop to think how far I have to haul that food?" And she would respond, "If you were downright hungry and in their place like that, wouldn't you have a kind feeling for someone if they would feed you?" He'd laugh and say, "You do follow the lessons of your Bible, Lizzie."

George followed the lessons of the Bible, as well, in terms of giving to others. He had a **steer** that had grown quite fat. He knew the Indians did not have enough to eat, so he offered the steer to them. They accepted it, but they were afraid to shoot it for fear of getting in trouble with the agency. (They were only allowed to kill a cow that belonged to them.)

So, George asked a hired man to kill the steer. The Indians then gathered around to skin it. When they were almost done, one offered Lizzie twenty-five cents for the intestines and stomach (which were highly prized by the Indians), but she would not accept the money, because she said the steer now belonged to the Indians themselves.

There were five Indian families there that day, so they divided the steer meat into five parts. Then they went to the creek to wash the intestines, and they strung a cord from one of their wagons to another. They sliced the meat as thinly as possible and hung it over the cord to dry. They blew air into the intestines to dry them, and then they cooked them to eat.

In October 1887, Lizzie went back to Iowa to give birth to another son, Carl. He was born on November 15th and was nicknamed Charlie.

When Thanksgiving came, since Lizzie was still in Iowa, George made a special dinner for the cowboys. He was not a skilled cook but he did his best. He later told her the only wild animal that had come around was a porcupine. So, George shot it, skinned it, stuffed it with bread dressing, and roasted it like a turkey. It looked okay but it tasted terrible! He and the men tried to enjoy it, but soon gave up and instead ate some dried beef for Thanksgiving dinner.

The men could not wait for Lizzie to come back and Lizzie felt the same. She looked forward to her return to life on the ranch and to the next visit by her friend, Sitting Bull.

# CHAPTER SEVEN – DESSERT FIRST (1888)

In the spring of 1888, Lizzie returned to the Dakotas with little John and newborn Charlie. Tillie still remained in Iowa with her grandparents, quite content in their care. It was the only life she had ever known, and her parents agreed that their ranch life in the wilderness, living around cowboys, was not appropriate for a little girl.

George always had a surprise for Lizzie when she returned to the ranch from Iowa. But this time the surprise was not very nice.

As their neighbor "Virginia Bill" Hamilton later related the tale, while Lizzie was back in Iowa, George had caught a little lamb and put it in the guest bedroom. He wanted to keep it long enough to show the cute little animal to "Virginia Bill." When George and "Virginia Bill" opened the bedroom door, their attention was first drawn to the cute little lamb.

But then they began to look around the room. The baby lamb had pooped a trail several times in a circle, each time crossing under the window and up over the two beds. Lizzie had left her nicest quilts on the beds, so George blurted out a swear word that should not be repeated. He then did his best to wash the quilts but they did not get as clean as he hoped they would. He had no choice but to tell Lizzie the tale after she came home.

Not long after Lizzie's return to the ranch, Sitting Bull came with some of his Lakota tribe for another visit. The Indians stopped their wagons, tied up their horses at the corral, and greeted Lizzie and George, the children, and the cowboys.

Grinding wheel

Then the Indians went to fill up their water pails. Each man, accompanied by his wife, carried an empty pail to the well. Once the pail was full, he would hand it to his wife to carry

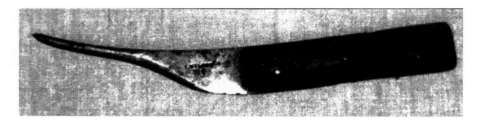

Knife gifted by Sitting Bull to George Dell

it to the house. While she toted the heavy pail, her husband politely walked along beside her.

Lizzie laughed at seeing this. In her experience among White people, a gentleman would usually offer to carry a heavy load for a lady. She quickly learned that the Indians had their own well-defined roles.

Next, the Indian men brought all their knives and hatchets up to the cabin. They never missed the opportunity to sharpen all of their blades on the sandstone grinding wheel that George had outside the cabin's front door.

On one of those occasions Sitting Bull gave George a small hunting knife. It had clearly been used for years to cut meat, as the blade was quite worn from being sharpened so frequently.

When they were finished sharpening their knives some of the Indian men went to the woodpile to fill a box with wood. They brought the wood to the kitchen so George could put more in the stove as needed. One of the Indian men filled the tea kettle with well water and set it back on top of the stove. Now that the preparations had been made, Lizzie knew it was time to serve the food.

Lizzie typically served them fried bacon, potatoes, bread, canned fruit, coffee, tea, and cookies, pies, or cake. Lizzie set out all the food along with dishes and spoons and the Indians got in a line to fill their plates. If there were more than eight Indians, they sat on the floor with their legs crossed.

The Indians' usual diet did not include sweets. Some of Sitting Bull's followers who had traveled with him in his shows tasted desserts for the first time at the elegant hotels where they stayed. Others discovered desserts for the first time at the Dells' house.

Sitting Bull had the biggest sweet tooth of them all.

When the Indians ate meals at the Dells', they liked to eat the desserts first. Lizzie always had pie, cake, or sugar cookies for them. Then they would eat their meat and potatoes. Sometimes they took sweets back to their tipis to give to the children, too.

And following the meal, George always brought out the sacred pipe for their friendship ritual.

In the summer of 1888, six wagons arrived at the Dells carrying at least twenty-five Indians.

Lizzie peeked out through the window curtains as the Indians climbed out of their wagons. She was alone in the house with the two little boys, while George and the men were on the range looking after the cattle.

Sitting Bull sometimes brought different members of his tribe when he visited, but Lizzie did not immediately recognize this group so she grew concerned. She also did not notice that Sitting Bull was in the group.

Also, at the time, tribes who were enemies of the Lakota were rumored to be in the area so George and the neighbors had been on the lookout.

Soon the group of Indians approached the cabin and began sharpening their knives and their hatchets on the grinding wheel near the front door.

Lizzie later said a woman left alone on a ranch in the wilderness could imagine almost anything when afraid. She knew that her fears were probably unfounded, yet she did not feel comfortable to welcome the strange Indians inside when George and the cowboys were not home. She later said that, had she known that her friend Sitting Bull was with the group, she would have felt differently.

The Indians began to knock on the front door.

Lizzie kept very still against an inside front wall so they would not know she was there, and she whispered to John to hide under a bed and be as quiet as a mouse. She held baby Charlie and rocked him in her arms to keep him asleep.

The living room grew dark as the Indians looked through the window, blocking the sunlight. After a while, the knocking stopped and the Indians got back in their wagons and pulled out. Lizzie sat down in her rocking chair and read her Bible to calm herself.

When George and his cowboys returned to the house later that day, she told them what had happened. The cowboys decided to ride out to search for the Indians to make sure they were Sitting Bull's people. They wanted to be certain the group of Indians were friendly and not to be feared by the homesteaders. Soon the cowboys came across some of the Standing Rock agency police and told them about the incident.

The Dells later heard that the agency police located the group of Indians, including Sitting Bull, that day and led them back to the Standing Rock Reservation. The Indians must have wondered what they had done to deserve the special police escort. But the incident also showed that while the homesteaders were personally acquainted with some Indians who were friendly, they also feared other native people who might want to harm them.

Lizzie had mixed feelings upon hearing that her mystery visitors turned out to have been Sitting Bull and some of his Lakota. She was glad that the Indians were his own group, but

88

## INDIAN AGENCY POLICE

These Indian police were hired by the Indian Agent to keep law and order on the reservation according to agency rules as well as state and federal laws (including the terms of treaties). Agents typically recruited these paid police from the reservation's tribe.

Pine Ridge Reservation Agency Police Chief, SD

sad that she had not realized it sooner to welcome them into the house.

During this period, Sitting Bull had increased his reputation across the country as the leader of all the Sioux nations. He also continued his pattern of resistance, which gained him even more attention.

In October 1888, the chief traveled to Washington, D.C., to plead with the US government to increase the beef allotment for the Sioux, because his people were starving. The government had cut the Indians' beef allotment in half. Officially, this was blamed on the expense; unofficially, it gave the government more bargaining power against the now starving Indians to take more of their native lands away.

Sitting Bull also spoke out against the government's decision to offer 11 million acres of reservation land for sale to the public for fifty cents an acre. He was part of a group of 67 Sioux chiefs, including fourteen from Standing Rock Reservation, who traveled to Washington accompanied by Agent McLaughlin. This was just part of a land-rights battle that had gone on for several years and would continue longer.

Not surprisingly, the visiting Indian chiefs made a big impression in the nation's capital. Reporters followed them wherever they went. The Indians visited the National Zoo and many of the museums of the Smithsonian Institution. They also posed for a group photo on the steps of the US Capitol Building.

Sitting Bull's influence was at its height. He even shook hands with President Benjamin Harrison while he was in Washington.

After he returned to the Dakota Territory, Sitting Bull took his people off the reservation on their fall hunt.

Sioux chiefs in Washington, DC

One Friday, Lizzie was making a rice pudding to have with their Sunday dinner, when George looked out the window and hollered to her, "Lizzie, your friends are coming."

Three wagons full of Indians came, and three more arrived not long after. Lizzie boiled water for potatoes, baked bread, and fried enough bacon to feed about 30 Indians. She put out all the desserts she had on hand this time, because she felt bad about how she had hidden from the group on their previous visit when she was afraid to welcome them into the house.

Later in the evening, George came back to the cabin from the Indians' camp and told Lizzie a baby had been born there that afternoon. He asked her if she would make a fruitcake and some coffee for the new mother.

Lizzie took the fruitcake and coffee to the camp the following morning and motioned to the Indian women that the food and drink were for the mother with the new baby. She cradled her arms as though she was holding a baby and rocked the imaginary baby back and forth. The women nodded and smiled, understanding the reason for the gift.

The next morning, one of the young Indian women knocked on the Dells' door. She brought Lizzie a hindquarter of deer, thanking her for Lizzie's gifts to the new mother. There was a saying at the time that an Indian never forgot a kindness, and George and Lizzie always found that to be true.

That afternoon, the Indians took down their tipis, packed up their wagons, and left for the reservation.

Lizzie took the hindquarter of deer and made dried meat like she had learned to do with beef in Iowa. She sliced the meat thinly and then placed it in a brine that she made from water, salt, black pepper, onions, and sugar. After brining the meat for several hours, she dried it with cloths and salted it again. Lizzie then hung the meat inside their smoke house behind the main cabin and smoked it over a wood fire for up to a month. Since dried meat could be stored for many months, this was a typical way to prepare a large amount of meat so that none ever went to waste.

Dr. Clemmer (George's business partner from Cresco, Iowa) often came to visit and proclaimed Lizzie's dried meat "the best he'd ever eaten in his life."

Lizzie also began planning another baking day. She would need to make more desserts for the couple's upcoming dinners with their cowboys and neighbors. Sitting Bull and his Indians had eaten up all the sweets in the house.

# CHAPTER EIGHT – THE COWS AND THE KISS (1889)

By this time, George and his cowboys had ranching down to a science.

The Triple-C cowboys and their neighbors rounded up the cattle twice a year. The cattle grazed on the prairie which had no fences so the cows became spread out for miles and all of them needed to be gathered together every spring and fall. In the spring, the cattle were rounded up for the **branding bee**. In the fall, they were rounded up so the cowboys could decide which cows were large enough to be sold for their meat.

Leading up to the fall roundup, George typically rode the range for up to 16 hours a day with 4 cowboys. Breakfast was at 3am so that they could be on their horses by daybreak. They searched high and low to find the cattle, and every day they collected more cattle into the corrals at the ranch to check their branding and hold for eventual shipment to the stock yards in Chicago.

Finally, all the ranchers in the area gathered for the fall roundup. George participated in this, but he preferred to let the young, experienced cowboys handle much of the work. Experienced cowboys excelled at herding, roping, branding, breaking horses, etc. Including the men from the Dell ranch, there were usually 40-to-50 cowboys on each roundup.

Each cowboy had ten to twelve horses (called cow ponies) to ride during the roundup. This was so that no single horse became too tired and also so that all the horses had plenty of time to eat grass to keep up their energy levels. Men called "horse watchmen" took care of all the cow ponies.

Branding calves 1900

Because the men could be working the roundup for months at a time, they traveled with a cook and a mess wagon.

During the fall roundup the men would decide which cows had reached the best weight for them to be sold in Chicago. Getting the cattle to the stockyards in Chicago was not easy. First came the roundup on the grazing lands. Then, once the men knew how many cows would be making the trip, rail cars had to be reserved to carry them (one rail car for every 22 cows).

### THE BRANDING BEE

In the late spring, the cattle were rounded up to be branded with the CCC (Triple C) brand. The cowboys would rope each calf or cow with a **lariat**, lay the animal on the ground and tie its legs together so it could not run away. Then the branding iron was heated in a fire and pressed into the animal's skin (usually on its side or on its back flank). The Dell's branding iron was only a single C so each poor cow had to be branded three times. The branding bee included all of the new calves that had been born that spring, as well as any cow that had been missed the previous year.

# THE CHUCK / MESS WAGON

Since the roundup took several weeks, a cook always traveled with them. His name was Louis Anderson and he was also the cook at the Ox Ranch, about forty miles away. Cowboys who worked for the Dells thought that Louis was a great cook and were impressed that he could also speak seven languages!

Louis drove the specially-designed chuck wagon (the food or "mess" wagon), which was pulled by a mule. Invented in 1866 by a Texas cattleman named Charles Goodnight, the chuck wagon was a great way to feed large numbers of men on a roundup.

The chuck wagon carried all the food supplies, cooking utensils, and a stove. On the back of the wagon was a large storage cabinet called a "chuck box," with a hinged door that folded down to serve as the cook's work table. Another storage space, called the "boot," held heavy items such as pots, frying pans, and a huge coffeepot.

Under the wagon a cowhide or canvas sling held wood and cow manure to fuel the cooking fire.

The front of the chuck wagon held food supplies such as flour, sugar, coffee, and canned goods (also called "airtights"), and could be covered with a waterproof canvas in bad weather.

A separate wagon held the men's personal items and clothing as well as all the bedding, which was brought out at night so the men could sleep under the stars.

Plans were also made to feed the cattle along the way so they arrived at the Chicago market at their perfect weight to be sold.

Because there were no fences, cattle from different ranches would often mix together. If another roundup group found one of your branded cows, they sent it off to market with their own. Because the cow had your brand on its hide, you would get the credit for the sale. When this happened a surprise check for the money would show up in your mail!

The ranchers banded together to drive all their cattle up north to the rail line in Dickinson. The trip took about ten days. Once the group got about ten miles from Dickinson, they held the cows there for a week or two. This allowed the cattle to graze until there were enough train cars in which to load them.

George met the group in Dickinson and then he and his neighboring ranchers traveled to Chicago with the cattle so they could sell them there. In Chicago, the trainline went straight to the Union Stockyards and employees there unloaded the cattle. George left his team of horses and the covered wagon in Dickinson until he returned from Chicago. The horses were cared for by the local **livery** [liv a rē]. After George left for Chicago on the train with the other ranchers and the cattle, his cowboys headed back to the ranch.

Lizzie ran the ranch when George was away. An old gold **prospector** they had befriended helped her with some of the daily duties and she felt safer with him there. The two of them were soon joined by the returning cowboys.

Once the cattle were sold in Chicago, George and his neighbors returned to Dickinson on the train. In Dickinson he bought provisions for the coming winter and loaded them up in the covered wagon before heading back to the ranch himself.

1883 was the first year that a shipment of cattle (from several Dakota Territory ranches) was sent from Dickinson by train to

Chicago's Union Stockyard. Records show that 1,219 train boxcars (pulled by several locomotive steam engines) held a total of 26,818 cows. The cows were sold in Chicago for $45 per cow—a total of $1,206,710 (over $30 million in today's dollars).

George Dell likely began to send his cattle to the Chicago Stockyards in 1885. It is not known how many cows were in his herd.

Today, Black Angus is the world's most common beef cattle breed. A single cow (depending upon its age, size, gender, and quality) may sell for $1,200 to $5,500.

In March 1889, Congress passed an act allowing the division of the Great Sioux Reservation into six smaller ones. It appeared that the US Government wanted to split the Sioux nations apart and take away more of their land.

This time the White men had finally gotten the number of signatures they needed from the Indian chiefs to pass the act. Most chiefs felt they had to sign, because many of the Indians were starving and the act promised to increase their food rations.

Although three fourths of the Indian chiefs signed the act, Sitting Bull refused to sign it. But that did not matter, because the Great Sioux Reservation would soon be nothing but a memory.

When a newspaper reporter asked Sitting Bull how the Indians felt about the agreement, he shouted "INDIANS! There are no INDIANS left but me!"

That summer, Sitting Bull came to the Dell ranch with six men including an interpreter, and the chief held a photo of himself in one hand. The photo had been taken in St. Paul, Minnesota, in 1884, and it showed his signature at the bottom.

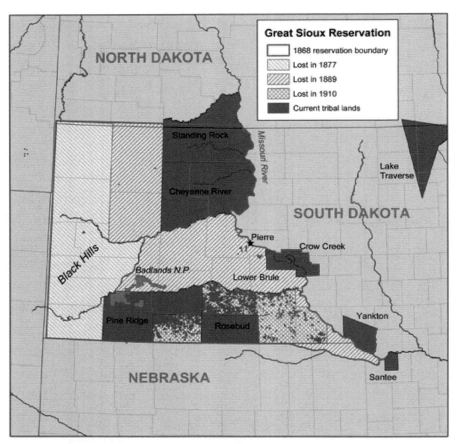

Depletion of the Great Sioux Reservation

Sitting Bull wanted to give the photo to Lizzie as a present because, the interpreter explained, she had been so kind to his people and always fed them whenever they came.

In exchange, Sitting Bull wanted a photo he had seen in the Dells' cabin. The photo showed Lizzie and her three children in front of her parents' farmhouse in Iowa.

Sitting Bull said that he wanted to hang Lizzie's photo up in the agency so he could show it to all his followers and tell them about her.

Lizzie agreed, and a broad smile crossed the chief's face. After they exchanged the photos, to Lizzie's great surprise Sitting Bull

Photo of Sitting Bull presented to Elizabeth Dell

leaned down and kissed her on the cheek. He then told her the women he met in Washington, D.C., the previous year had admired him very much and had begged him for a kiss on the cheek. Thus, he explained, Lizzie should consider it a great honor!

Lizzie glanced over at her husband who could hardly suppress a chuckle when he saw the shocked look on her face!

In August 1889, Sitting Bull predicted a bleak year ahead. He said the sun would burn up everything. The crops would all fail, and many of his people would starve. From the day of his prediction, no rain or snow fell at Standing Rock for the next ten months.

At the Triple-C Ranch, it was miserably hot and windy. Many settlers, experiencing the same bad **drought** [drout], gave up and fled back east to their home states like Iowa and Illinois. Although the Dakota cattle boom had finally turned into a bust, the Dells still remained on their ranch.

Lizzie Dell's tin button box

That fall, the Lakota returned to Bull Creek for their usual hunt. The Dells, including their children, John and Charlie, looked forward to Sitting Bull's visits. George frequently took John and Charlie to the Indians' camp on Bull Creek, or the Indian kids would come up to the Dell cabin. The boys played with the Lakota children every day the Indians were there.

The Dell children and the Lakota children used a broomstick to pretend to "ride horsey" like the adult cowboys and Indians. They also had a tobacco can full of buttons which they played games with by the hour. Additionally, George had put some sand near one corner outside the cabin, and all the kids loved to dig and play in it using baking powder cans as molds to build all sorts of things.

Nothing was more fun for the kids than hanging around the horse corral. It was like a constant wild west show, with calves being branded and new horses being broken so they could be ridden by the cowboys.

BREAKING A HORSE

"Breaking a horse" means to train it to be ridden and obey commands from the rider. At first, a young horse does not like a bit and bridle, the assembly of straps on its head and a metal bit in its mouth to control the horse's actions. A young horse also does not like the weight and feel of a saddle, especially with a rider, on its back. Once the horse gets accustomed to all this and is considered safe to ride, the horse is called "broken."

Horse Corral

In the spring, all the cow ponies had to have horseshoes put on so they would be ready for working on the spring roundups of new calves. The horseshoes protected the horses' hooves from wear and damage and also provided good traction on the hilly and sometimes slippery ground. In the fall, the horseshoes were removed before the ponies were put out to pasture; a "barefoot" hoof was (and still is) considered a healthy option for most non-working horses.

Lizzie and George home-schooled their children together at the ranch. Along with other subjects, George taught the boys their multiplication tables using match sticks, and Lizzie taught the children to speak German, since that was the language she had first spoken in Prussia before emigrating to America. George was a loving but strict father; he required the children to speak German with their mother and English with him so they would learn both languages. Once when a German cowboy visited the Dells, he spoke to two-year-old Charlie in German, and was surprised when Charlie replied back to him in perfect German.

As the year 1889 came to a close, it would be remembered by Dakota homesteaders as the year the Dakota Territory was officially to become two separate states, North and South Dakota, the 39th and 40th states of the Union (finalized in 1890). Of course, Lizzie would always remember 1889 as the year she received an unexpected kiss from the famous Chief Sitting Bull. She could never forget it, especially since George kidded her about it for years to come.

# CHAPTER NINE –
# THE WORST YEAR EVER (1890)

The year 1890 was a bad year for the Dell family. In May, their youngest son, Charlie, fell ill with pneumonia, and there were no doctors within a hundred miles of the ranch.

A visiting cowboy suggested a **poultice** [pōl tes] made of boiled potato skins and dirt be put on Charlie's chest and throat. But it was of no use, or perhaps it was just too late. Sadly, Charlie died at age two and a half after a week-long illness.

George and Lizzie were devastated. Charlie's death was a deep blow to the couple, who wondered if things might have turned out differently if they had left the boy back in Iowa with Lizzie's parents and his little sister, Tillie. They were so heartbroken they even thought that maybe they should never have come to the Dakotas in the first place.

Following the death of their son, the Dells took their wagon to Camp Crook, the closest town thirty miles away, to buy some good quality lumber to build a child-sized casket. They lined it with white muslin cloth and buried Charlie in it up on a little butte a half mile west of their house, within sight of the cabin.

Because the neighboring ranchers lived many miles away, they did not know about Charlie's death in time for his short funeral service. Only the Dells and their cowboys were in attendance. Of course, Charlie's older brother, John, who would turn four years old in a few months, did not understand why his little brother had gone up to heaven. He felt very sad and lonely without him.

Butte where Carl Dell was buried

According to future landowners, local ranchers did not forget Charlie. For decades afterward, they took flowers up to the butte on Memorial Day in honor of the boy they called "the little angel."

The summer after Charlie's death, Sitting Bull and his Lakota arrived at the Dell ranch with their usual gifts of animal hides and new moccasins for Lizzie, John, and Charlie.

When they asked where Charlie was, Lizzie pointed up to heaven. When the Indians realized Charlie was dead, they would not let her keep the moccasins that had been made especially for him.

Lizzie was sad. She had hoped to have the tiny beaded shoes in memory of Charlie, and she could not understand why the Indians refused to let her have them. George later reasoned that perhaps the Lakota had a belief that prevented them from leaving a gift for a deceased person.

Later that summer, Lizzie became pregnant again. She and George were thrilled at first; however, the Dells' string of bad luck that year continued.

In early fall, Lizzie and their son, John, were involved in a bad accident. The two of them were traveling in their buckboard wagon to visit a sick neighbor. As they started down a hill, something startled the horses, probably a rattlesnake.

The horses reared up, and Lizzie and John were both thrown off the wagon. John seemed unhurt but Lizzie was very shaken. She later believed the trauma of the accident caused her to have a miscarriage that night. She had sadly lost two children in six months—first Charlie and now her unborn baby.

Following the miscarriage, Lizzie remained ill for several days. Since there were no doctors nearby to help her, she simply tried to rest until she felt better. The cowboys took four-year-old John out on their horses during the days so the cabin would be quiet for her.

George prepared beef tea for her from this recipe in one of their cookbooks:

One pound of lean beef, cut into small pieces. Put into a jar. Cover the jar tightly and place it in a pot of cold water. Heat the water gradually to a boil, and continue this steadily for three or four hours, until the meat looks like white rags, and the juice is all drawn out. Throw the meat out, season the juice with salt, and when cooled, skim off any fat.

Lizzie believed a daily dose of George's beef tea along with a strong will to live helped her to recover. When she finally began feeling better, she decided she would take young John to Iowa for the winter.

The Lakota had grown more desperate than ever. They struggled every day with disease, starvation, and hopelessness.

Letters came to the Lakota leaders from Indian chiefs in the American southwest about an Indian in the state of Nevada named Wovoka [woe-voe-ka], who claimed to have had a message from God, in a vision, that the Indians must give up their warlike ways. In return, he claimed, they would be rewarded with wonderful lives, with plenty of buffalo and with freedom from sickness, death, and White people.

Wovoka explained that the Indians must also perform a special ritual, a "Ghost Dance" in order to bring about this vision of the future. Ghost dancers wore white shirts or robes made from flour sacks. He told them to put their weapons and guns aside and to dance peacefully.

Several Sioux leaders (not including Sitting Bull), traveled to Nevada over the winter to seek out Wovoka to learn more about his vision. According to one of the Sioux delegates, Good Thunder, Wovoka showed them the dance and told them about his vision. Good Thunder said that Wovoka could also read the Sioux leaders' thoughts and answer them without words.

Wovoka was believed by many to be a **messiah** of the new religion. Variations of the Ghost Dance were soon performed by Indian nations across the American West and Midwest, including the Lakota. By 1890 many Indians felt so hopeless they believed the Ghost Dance was their only chance for survival.

However, most White people wanted to stop the dancing, because they did not understand it and many were afraid of what it might make the Indians do. Some of the Indians even implied they might resort to violence if the White people tried to stop them from performing the Ghost Dance.

Some Indians at the Standing Rock Reservation began participating in the Ghost Dance. Even though Sitting Bull did not join them, he allowed the dances to continue, out of concern for his followers, because he saw that it gave them hope for a better future.

By October 1890, the US military was trying to find out where the Ghost Dance was occurring and who was participating. Sitting Bull declared he was ready to fight and die if the military attempted to stop the Ghost Dance, because faith in the dance's power had become almost like a religion to his people.

That same month, Elaine Goodale, the reservation's supervisor of education, invited Sitting Bull to her tipi on the reservation for dinner one night. Sitting Bull's nephew was Elaine's carriage driver, and he had arranged for the two to meet. Sitting Bull refused to discuss the new religion of the Ghost Dance with her when she brought up the topic. Sitting Bull did, however, smilingly profess to Miss Goodale his "warm friendship for the White people."

Standing Rock Agent James McLaughlin told the Commissioner of Indian Affairs in Washington, D.C., that Sitting Bull was the real power behind the "evil" Ghost Dance religion. Yet, Sitting Bull had neither participated in nor directed the Ghost Dance.

Regardless, the situation escalated.

The year 1890 had been a bad one for the Lakota Indians, as well. Because of the US government's orders to kill the buffalo, the animals were long gone as the Indians' primary means of food, warmth, and tools. Also, from August 1889 to June 1890 there had been no rain, so the crops that the Lakota had been taught to plant on the reservation had failed. There was much sickness; whooping cough, measles, and influenza had killed many of the Lakota tribe's members. In addition, the beef rations issued to the Lakota Sioux had been cut by Congress, and the Indians were hungry again. Many Lakota were dying of starvation, especially the weakest of them—the elderly and the children.

By that fall, rumors began to circulate that the Sioux were getting restless and preparing to attack White people on nearby farms and villages. By September, newspapers printed stories (many false) about Lakota attacks, stories that added to the White people's fears. Some pioneers fled their homes or moved from their farms and ranches into small towns for their safety. The government and the newspapers wrongly reported that the great Lakota chief, Sitting Bull, was behind these attacks against the White people.

George felt that it was time for Lizzie and four-year-old John to return to Iowa until the "Indian situation" improved.

He would travel with them on their small buckboard wagon, pulled by two of their horses. Their destination was the town of Dickinson, where Lizzie and John could take the train to Cresco, Iowa, while George returned to their cattle ranch alone. Lizzie planned to spend the winter in Iowa with John and her daughter, Tillie.

Lizzie and George's neighbors pleaded with them not to leave, because the Indians in the area were now thought to be on the war path. The ranchers warned the couple that they and their young son might not survive the three-day journey across the prairie. But Lizzie and George insisted upon leaving.

## ON THE WARPATH

The warpath was literally the "path to war" taken by American Indians when traveling to an enemy's territory to engage in battle.

Not long into their trip George and Lizzie noticed a man on horseback in the distance, outlined against the horizon. He was close enough that they could tell by the color of his skin that he was an Indian. Their neighbors' warnings rushed back to them. Had they put themselves and their son in danger?

The Indian did not approach them that day, but he rode where he could keep them in view, and George and Lizzie would often catch sight of him on the high ridges alongside their route.

Who was this Indian, and what did he want with the pioneer couple? Lizzie and George knew that the Indians were lately growing angry and restless because their people were starving. Their situation was quite desperate and George and Lizzie had felt nothing but sympathy for them.

Despite the fact that the Indian stranger seemed to be following them, Lizzie maintained her confidence about the couple's friendship with the local Lakota tribe. She refused to be afraid, despite their neighbors' warnings.

That night, Lizzie pulled the blankets up under her chin in the back of the wagon. It was pitch black outside and so quiet that every tiny sound startled her. She was exhausted though, and finally drifted off to sleep.

She dreamed of their little girl, Tillie. Lizzie dearly missed her and was looking forward to spending time with her. Tillie was hundreds of miles away in Cresco, Iowa, and Lizzie and George had seen her only a few times in the little girl's six years. After losing two of the couple's children earlier that year, Lizzie yearned to spend time with the two who remained.

George gently shook Lizzie awake early the next morning. They prepared a fire, made their coffee, and ate a breakfast of dried meat and canned fruit that Lizzie had packed for the trip. The

Indian on the horse was nowhere to be seen. And yet, they knew they had not imagined him. Where had he gone?

The family finished eating and then continued toward Dickinson. But before long they could, again, sense the Indian's presence nearby. Not wanting to say anything in front of little John, who sat between them on the wagon's bench seat, the couple communicated their concern through their facial expressions. George and Lizzie were puzzled. They kept wondering who the Indian was and why he was following them.

The Indian lingered behind them for three days all the way to Dickinson. He came quite close on the day the Dells arrived in Dickinson, and they could then see that he had the high cheekbones and broad face of the Lakota. The handsome young man looked similar to the Indians they had met from the Lakota tribe.

George and Lizzie finally realized why the mysterious Indian had been tailing them the entire time. The young Lakota must have been one of Sitting Bull's followers, who was escorting them to make certain that they would not be harmed by any other Indian tribes on their journey. George and Lizzie thought that the Indian escort must surely have been provided by their friend Sitting Bull himself, who had ordered him to keep a close eye on the Dell family as they traveled to Dickinson. Sitting Bull wanted to ensure the family would be safe as they crossed the prairie. There was no other explanation.

Later, George and Lizzie would sadly understand that the protective watch of this stranger whom Lizzie would forever after call "our escort in the distance" was Chief Sitting Bull's final gift to them. It was also a sign that the great chief truly valued the Dells' friendship as much as they did his. Sadly, though, they would never see their friend Sitting Bull again.

Soon, the US government, along with newspapers across the country, targeted Sitting Bull as the instigator of the Ghost Dance movement and began a widespread campaign against him. Government officials ordered the Indian agent McLaughlin to arrest Sitting Bull on the upcoming date, December 20th. But on December 13th, Sitting Bull told McLaughlin that he was planning to leave Standing Rock Reservation in a few days to join the Ghost Dancers at the Pine Ridge Reservation south of there, with or without McLaughlin's permission. McLaughlin decided to move quickly and place Sitting Bull under arrest sooner than he had originally planned.

In the early morning on December 15th, the Indian agency police, with the US Army's support, arrived at Sitting Bull's cabin to place him under arrest. It was dark outside and an icy drizzle filled the air. "Brother, we have come after you," one of the Indian police, a Lakota, stated in a harsh voice after stepping into the cabin. Sitting Bull quietly replied, "All right." Having just awoken, Sitting Bull peacefully submitted to the arrest and asked the men to saddle his favorite horse, Rico, the gray one that Buffalo Bill had given him.

The Indian police were reportedly nervous about arresting the great chief. They clumsily shoved Sitting Bull and each other around in the process. They tried to push Sitting Bull toward the front door of his cabin while he was still naked. The chief reportedly said, "This is a great way to do things, not to give me a chance to put on my clothes in wintertime."

By the time they let him dress and led him outside, other Lakota in the area had gathered in his support. In the confusion of the crowd, including Sitting Bull's two wailing wives, and barking packs of dogs, Sitting Bull's teenage son, Crow Foot, scolded his father. "You always call yourself a brave chief. Now you are allowing yourself to be taken...."

Upon hearing his son's words, Sitting Bull had a sudden change of heart. He shouted out his resistance to the arrest and threw his captors' hands off him. One of his supporters fired a gun at one of the policemen, then multiple shots were fired. Sitting Bull was killed instantly, along with seven of his followers, including his son, Crow Foot. Six of the Indian police were also killed.

When Rico heard the shots, he reared up on his hind legs and waved a front hoof in the air, as he had been trained to do in Buffalo Bill's show. When the Indian police saw this, they reportedly thought Sitting Bull's soul had entered the horse's body and they seemed afraid.

Later that day, an estimated 500 Lakota quietly slipped away from the reservation and scattered to unknown locations. While they were almost powerless before, the death of their chief must have left them entirely hopeless and afraid.

"Virginia Bill" Hamilton told how he and the other homesteaders were also frightened soon after Sitting Bull's death. They had heard that the Lakota were wild with anger about their chief's death and had gone "on the war path." Some of the cowboys from the area headed for the Black Hills, where US officials were giving free guns to the ranchers so they could defend themselves against the potential Indian threat. The cowboys agreed to gather back at the Dell ranch once they had picked up their guns.

"Virginia Bill" rounded up all the men he could find and headed for the Dell ranch six miles away from his own ranch. When the men arrived, they found no one else there. The horses and cows had been let loose, which was done only in a real emergency.

Thinking they had made a mistake about the meeting place the men went on to Joe Johnson's ranch few miles away. No one was there either, and they saw that the livestock had been let loose, like at the Dell ranch. Inside the Johnson house, things were in disarray as though people had left in a hurry. A half-eaten supper was still on the table and chairs had been knocked over.

The group of armed men went another four miles to Alec Connell's ranch. No one was there either, but the house seemed in order. And again, there were no cattle or horses anywhere to be seen.

The men eventually split up and continued on to different ranches. Some decided to stay at Johnson's ranch overnight and take turns sleeping and keeping watch. Soon, the watchmen thought they spotted some Indians sneaking up on the ranch behind some large boulders so they woke the other men and fled for their lives.

After riding forty miles at top speed, they finally felt safe enough to stop and rest. They were embarrassed to later figure out that the creatures "sneaking up" on the ranch behind the rocks were probably just some grazing cows, not hostile Indians. Even the men who had been keeping guard admitted this was likely the truth.

It turned out the ranchers who had let their animals loose had done so in order to save them. Letting them loose would enable the animals to run away if they sensed danger. The ranchers knew from experience the horses and cattle would return home once the danger passed and they grew hungry.

Rumors spread quickly about the Indians' possible belligerent behavior. White people in the closest towns heard a fake rumor that all the ranchers in the Cave Hills had been killed by the Indians that week.

But not one White person in the area had been killed by a Lakota, and many of the ranchers there felt sorry for the Indians because, like for the Dell family, 1890 had been the worst year ever for the Lakota, too.

SIOUX TRIBES AND BANDS

The Sioux Nation has historically been classified into three dialects of the Sioux language, Lakota, Nakota, and Dakota. Each of these has multiple tribes (for example, Santee, Teton, Yankonai), and bands (for example, Oglala, the band that Chief Crazy horse belonged to, and Hunkpapa, the band of Chief Sitting Bull). Tribes and bands are also sometimes referred to as "nations."

# CHAPTER TEN - ALL THE DREAMS DIED (1891-1896)

Sitting Bull spent most of his adult life defending his people and their way of life. He once said, "No man controls our footsteps. If we must die, we die defending our rights."

His death and the events leading up to it were immediately reported in newspapers across the country. Since Lizzie was back in Iowa at the time, it is not known how she heard about his death. She could have read about it in the newspaper or heard about it from family and friends in Cresco. Since George was at the ranch at the time, he probably quickly learned of Sitting Bull's death through word of mouth.

By the new year, the Lakota were mourning the loss of many more of their people. On December 29th, two weeks after Sitting Bull's death, the US Cavalry slaughtered a great number of Lakota, possibly including some of Sitting Bull's followers, in the **Massacre** [mas a ker] at Wounded Knee.

Wounded Knee was the name of a creek on the Pine Ridge Indian Reservation, which is in the southern part of South Dakota. The army had gone there to take away the Indians' weapons. In the process, one of the Indians' guns fired off, and that sparked a violent attack by the US military.

The cavalry immediately fired in a frenzy upon the Lakota, killing or mortally wounding about 300 of them. Two thirds of the victims were women and children, including infants in their mothers' arms. After much shooting had gone on, little Indian children were told by the soldiers, "It's OK to come out

115

now. We won't hurt you." But when the children came out from their hiding places, they were shot to death. Some Indian women who ran away were chased for miles and gunned down by the Army on horseback.

The Massacre at Wounded Knee became the symbol of the end of American Indians' freedom. Black Elk, the medicine man of Crazy Horse's Oglala Lakota, sadly said, "A people's dream died there."

Following Sitting Bull's death and the Massacre at Wounded Knee, life for the Lakota Indians became even more difficult; jobs were scarce, housing was poor, and there was not enough food to go around.

When Lizzie and George reunited again at the ranch in the spring of 1891, they mourned for the death of their friend, Sitting Bull. They also shared the anger many White people felt about the circumstances of Sitting Bull's death. The couple had grown fond of Sitting Bull over the past few years and felt he had grown fond of them as well.

The Dells later said they might have been the only two White people Sitting Bull really ever trusted. The history books now tell us there were a few others, but the great chief could probably have counted them on one hand.

Sitting Bull's followers continued to visit Lizzie and George for five more years until the Dells moved back to Iowa in 1896. Lizzie and George treated the Lakota with the same respect as they had when the great chief was with them.

The Indians brought animal skins and newly-beaded moccasins as gifts, as they always had done. They pitched their tipis, drew buckets of water from the well, and ate their meals with the Dells, just like in old times.

Over the years these Indians had become the Dells' friends. Lizzie and George had known many of them for a decade since Sitting Bull's first visit and had watched their children grow up and start new families. This new generation of Indians was increasingly learning English, and they liked to speak with George and Lizzie about memories of their beloved Chief Sitting Bull.

By the mid-1890s, cattle ranching in South Dakota had become increasingly difficult. The prairie grasses were being depleted by the cattle, and the wolf population was increasing. At the same time, cattle prices were dropping. This prompted George and Lizzie to end their dream of becoming successful cattle ranchers. They sold their homestead and returned to their families in Cresco, Iowa.

In 1895, they built a new, larger house on George's 160 acres near Davis Corners and began to live and work again as farmers.

Dell Farmhouse near Cresco, Iowa. Lizzie, Ellen, Walter, Lizzie's mother, Mathilde, circa 1903

Their two-story farmhouse must have seemed like a palace to Lizzie compared to their rustic log cabin in South Dakota.

The Dells never regretted their rich experiences as Dakota homesteaders. They were forever grateful for the many friends they had made there, including Chief Sitting Bull and his followers.

They also missed the vast, rugged Dakota prairie and—as their former neighbor "Virginia Bill" had once described—"how brightly the sun, moon, and stars did shine there."

Lizzie and George especially missed their son, Charlie, and knew they might never be able to return to South Dakota to visit his gravesite. Lizzie would sometimes close her eyes and picture in her mind a lone man slowing his horse in respect as he passed that peaceful butte where Charlie was buried. She may have imagined him a Cave Hills' cowboy or maybe a young Lakota man like the one who had escorted them safely to the train station many years ago.

Sitting Bull's survivors surely missed the wisdom and strength of their chief. However, even though he gained his people's respect for his resistance to the ways of the White man, Sitting Bull had come to realize he and his followers must eventually change with the times. He hadn't given up, but rather compromised for the future of his children.

In the last years of his life, Sitting Bull had actively sought to learn the ways of the White people he had professed to hate. His trust of Lizzie and George and his willingness to build a friendship with them is evidence of his intent to embrace his changing world. And the Dells' friendship with Chief Sitting Bull broadened their own world and changed their lives forever.

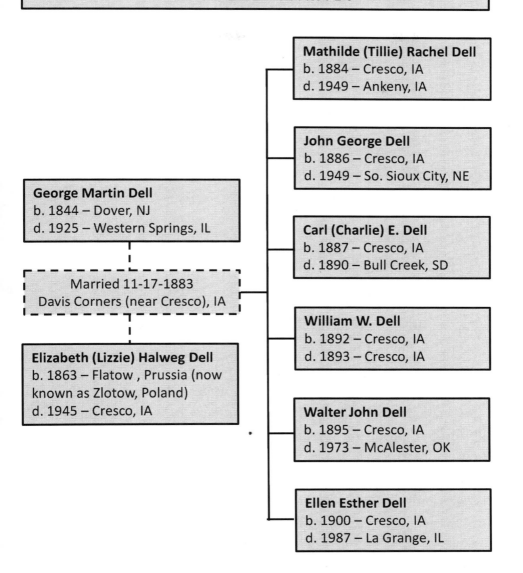

# EPILOGUE – THE DELLS AND THE LAKOTA TODAY

Descendants of the Dells and their families live all over the United States and beyond. Many of their great-grandchildren are in touch through ancestry websites, online meetings, and family reunions. For almost eighty years, our families have visited the site of the Dell ranch near Buffalo, South Dakota, and the Dell's 1890s farm near Cresco, Iowa.

We all grew up hearing the stories in this book and are proud that our ancestors knew and befriended such an influential man as Chief Sitting Bull.

Since the 1930s, our family has researched pieces of the story. Most of us have extensively read about Sitting Bull, his life, and the plight of the Lakota.

Certain family members have taken great interest in the Sheffield hunting knife and hand-made pipe acquired from Sitting Bull by George Dell. A granddaughter recalls taking the knife to school for "show and tell" during the 1930s. Several family members have visited Pipestone, MN, to see the Sioux quartzite and pipestone quarries and learn about the pipe-making process.

Many Dell descendants have somehow contributed to American Indian interests. The Dell's youngest daughter, Ellen, born in 1900 after their Dakota days, knitted dozens of mittens and shipped them to Standing Rock Reservation children for decades. Her daughter, Dode, gave a sizable donation to the Smithsonian's Museum of the American Indian, which opened in 2005. Ellen's other daughter, Jean, wrote a well-researched

120

book for our family in 2005 and our newest generations continue to show interest in learning about the Lakota and the friendship between the Dells and Chief Sitting Bull.

In 1990, both houses of the US Congress passed a resolution on the historical centennial (100-year anniversary) of the killings at Wounded Knee, formally expressing "deep regret" for the massacre.

Today, more than 70,000 Lakota live on and off reservations, and unfortunately many of them live in poverty. The majority of the estimated 35,000 who live on reservations live on the Pine Ridge Reservation in southern South Dakota. Most of Pine Ridge is located in the poorest county in the United States, Oglala Lakota County. The estimated unemployment rate there is 90%, the school dropout rate is 70%, much of the population is in poor health, and the average life expectancy is much lower than overall American averages.

Standing Rock Reservation, where Chief Sitting Bull lived, still straddles the border between North and South Dakota. Its population of less than 10,000 Lakota and Dakota struggles with the same poverty issues as Pine Ridge.

However, many Lakota also have the opportunity to go to college to learn to become teachers, doctors, lawyers, and other professionals. Others have continued to farm or raise cattle where their ancestors once hunted buffalo.

There is a revival of Lakota traditions and the Lakota language. Many Lakota practice the customs of their ancestors including native dancing, horseback riding, and creative and fine arts. The Lakota Language Consortium seeks to preserve the unique Lakota language.

Today, Chief Sitting Bull is remembered in classrooms and museums across America. Students can attend Sitting Bull

College in North Dakota, whose motto is a quote from Sitting Bull, "Let us put our minds together and see what life we can make for our children." It's a good motto for all of us to follow.

# ACKNOWLEDGMENTS

This book would not have been possible without my amazing family! First, Lizzie and George's youngest daughter, Ellen Dell Bieler, my Great Aunt Ellen, who read her mother's journals and wisely interviewed Lizzie in the 1930s to fill in the blanks. Next, Ellen's daughter, Jean Bieler Hastings, who enriched the story with its historical context and then shared her version with our entire family in 2005. Last, Lizzie's grandson, John Hamilton Radcliffe, my Dad, for mesmerizing us with our great-grandparents' pioneer adventures.

Heartfelt thanks to the Jim Clarkson family near Buffalo, South Dakota, for letting my family visit the old Dell ranch site now on the Clarkson Ranch for over eighty years and also to farmer John Casey of Cresco, Iowa for graciously allowing us on several occasions to poke around the old Dell farmhouse, barn, and outbuildings now located on his land.

Thank you to my siblings, Dell, Jay, and Lisa, and to our dear cousins, the Dell's granddaughters Jean Hastings and Dode Barker and great-granddaughters Heather Cassidy, Heidi Hastings, and Sharon Hudgins for sharing this fun adventure with us!

Thank you to Des Moines Findley Elementary 5th grade teachers Erin Budreau and Bob Williams and to your students for letting me share some of this story with you! The students' curiosity and enthusiasm about the Dells and Sitting Bull encouraged me to complete this book!

This is my first book and I quickly learned that, like many of life's most rewarding endeavors, it took a village! A special thank you to author and consultant Kali White VanBaale, whose thoughtful early suggestions have been incorporated into a better-flowing book. A huge thank you to Jan Davison, as well, for her thoughtful and professional editing. Sharon Hudgins, my cousin, graciously provided a very thorough (and free!) final edit. Special thanks to my voluntary early readers, whose help and advice I have appreciated so much: Heather Cassidy, Mike Delaney, Bill Dunlop, Eugene Fracek, Mollie and David Francis, M. Louise Gately, Phyllis Goodman, Heidi Hastings, Jean Hastings, Madison Keoouthai, Deb McHose, Jane Olson, Dell Radcliffe, Carol Riley, and Alex Slack. Thanks to artist Scott Stouffer who sketched the map of Sitting Bull's travels as conceptualized by my sister, Dell Radliffe. Lastly, a big shout out to Steve Semken, owner of Ice Cube Press, who not only patiently and expertly turned my manuscript into a real book, but also designed its striking cover!

And, thanks to you, dear reader, for your interest in our family's story!

# GLOSSARY

Alkali – bitter minerals not suitable for drinking

Ancestors – people who were members of one's family long ago, like grandparents and great-grandparents

Badlands – an area of South Dakota characterized by unusual rock formations

Black Angus – a Scottish breed of beef cattle

Black Hills – a small mountain range in South Dakota covered with trees and which looks black from a distance (considered sacred to the Lakota)

Branded – past tense of brand, to burn a mark onto an animal's hide with a hot branding iron, to identify to whom the animal belongs

Branding bee – an event where cowboys from nearby ranches gather together to help with one another's cattle branding

Buckboard – a four-wheeled, open carriage pulled by oxen or horses

Buttes [byoots] – hills that rise sharply from the land and have a flat top

Calico – cotton cloth with a printed pattern

Cavalry [ka val rē] – military troops historically on horseback (now in armored vehicles)

Colonel [ker nal] – a military officer ranking just below a general

Cradleboards – wooden frames worn on the back, used by many northern American Indian women for carrying infants

Dakota Territory – the former US territory that became the states North and South Dakota in 1890

Demise – end, death

Drought [drout] – a long period when there is little or no rain in a region

Finale [fa nal li] – the last part of a show or a piece of music

Field glass – a small portable telescope used outdoors

Freight wagon – a wagon used on the stagecoach roads for transporting products such as food and lumber

Homesteaders – settlers who live on land granted to them by the government

Lance – a long spear used for fighting on horseback

Lariat – a lasso made of rope

Livery [liv a rē] – a place that rents horse stables

Lye – a very strong cleaning solution made from wood ashes and water

Manifest Destiny – the idea that the United States White population had the God-given right to take over the entire country, from sea to sea

Massacre [mas a ker] – the brutal killing of many people or animals

Medic – a military hospital assistant

Messiah – a deliverer of a message and/or a liberator of people

Moccasins – soft, flat-soled Indian shoes or slippers made from deer hides

Nation – a self-governed group of people who share the same leadership, customs, and laws

Nomadic – pertaining to people who move around a large area (usually to find food), instead of living only in one place

Pockmarked – a mark, pit, or depressed scar left by smallpox or acne

Poultice [pōl tes] – a soft, moist, mass of material applied to the body to relieve illness

Prospector – a person who searched an area for gold, oil, or other valuable mineral deposits

Provisions – supplies of food that can be stored

Quarry [kwor-ē] – an open pit that is a source of stone, or to cut stone from that pit

Quinine [kwi nine] – a bitter substance made from tree bark and used as a medicine

Reservation agent – a person assigned by the government to manage an Indian reservation

Reservations – lands reserved by the government for the American Indians to live on

Robes – the furry hides of buffalo used for blankets or rugs

Sinew [sin you] – animal tendon that joins a muscle to a bone, used by American Indians as sewing thread

Six shooters – guns sometimes called revolvers with six bullet chambers

Stagecoach – a carriage with four wheels that is pulled by a team of horses, once used to carry mail and passengers

Steer – a young, male cow raised especially for beef

Tableaus [tah blōs] – a group of motionless figures representing a scene from a story or from history

Tanned – past tense of tan: the process of making leather out of an animal hide

Trading posts – stores where money or local products such as furs or hides are exchanged for manufactured goods or supplies

Travois [tra voy] – a type of sled formerly used by some American Indians to carry goods, consisting of two joined poles dragged by a horse or dog

Treaties – official agreements between two or more countries, governments, or rulers

War bonnet – a American Indian headdress consisting of a headband with a crown and tail of ornamental feathers, often eagle feathers. Each feather was awarded for a feat of battle courage, thus the chiefs wore full headdresses with dozens of feathers

Warrior – one engaged or experienced in battle

Washboard – a board with a ridged wood or metal surface used for scrubbing clothes against when washing them

# BIBLIOGRAPHY

Alderson, Nannie T. and Smith, Helena Huntington. *A Bride Goes West*. Lincoln, NE: Buffalo Books, University of Nebraska Press, 1942.

Brown, Dee. *Bury My Heart at Wounded Knee: An Indian History of the American West*. New York, NY: Bantom Books, 1970.

Eastman, Elaine Goodale. *Sister to the Sioux: The Memoirs of Elaine Goodale Eastman*, 1885-1891. Lincoln, NE: University of Nebraska Press, 1978.

Greene, Jerome A. *American Carnage: Wounded Knee, 1890*. University of Oklahoma Press, Norman Publishing Division, 2014.

Hamilton, W. H. *Dakota: An Autobiography of a Cowman*. Pierre, SD: South Dakota Historical Society Press, South Dakota Historical Collections, Volume 19, 1938.

Hastings, Jean Bieler. *Homesteading in South Dakota 1883-1895: Elizabeth and George Dell*. Madison, WI: Published by the author, 2005.

Hudgins, Sharon. "Home on the Range: Chuckwagons on the Ranch and on the Trail," New York, NY: *Saveur Magazine*, 2009.

Hudgins, Sharon. "A Prussian Pioneer on America's Last Frontier," *German Life magazine* (USA), LaVale, MD: Zeitgeist Publishing, June/July 2016, pp. 40-43.

LaPointe, Ernie (Great-Grandson of Sitting Bull). *Sitting Bull: His Life and Legacy*. Gibbs Smith, 2009.

McLaughlin, James. *My Friend the Indian*. Published by the author in 1910.

Nerburn, Kent. *Neither Wolf Nor Dog: On Forgotten Roads with an Indian Elder*. Novato, CA: New World Library, 1994.

Roosevelt, Theodore, and Frederic Remington. *Ranch Life in the Far West*. Outing, MN: Northland Press, 1968.

Utley, Robert M. *Sitting Bull: The Life and Times of an American Patriot*. New York, NY: Henry Holt and Company, 1993.

Vestal, Stanley. *Sitting Bull: Champion of the Sioux*. Boston, MA: Houghton Mifflin Company, 1932.

# ART AND PHOTO CREDITS
(by page number)

Courtesy of Library of Congress = LOC
Courtesy of Wikipedia = W
Courtesy of Jean Bieler Hastings = JBH
Courtesy of the Southwestern North Dakota Digital Archive at the
Dickinson Museum Center – DMCDADMC = DMC

11. Sitting Bull with one feather (LOC)
18. American Bison (W)
20. James McLaughlin (W)
25. St. Paul, MN firehouse (LOC)
26. Map of travel route (JBH)
26. Black angus cows (LOC)
28. River ferry crossing (LOC)
29. Typical pioneers (LOC)
31. Washboard (W: Yannick Trottier)
32. Badlands (photo by author)
34. Fording the river (courtesy of M. Louise Gately)
35. Map of Dell homestead location in the Cave Hills (courtesy of
    Custer National Forest, Sioux Division, Montana and SD, 1938,
    USDA Forest Service, and JBH)
37. Deadwood Stagecoach (DMC)
37. Floorplan Cabin #1 (JBH)
39. Bull Creek (photo by author)
42. Annie Oakley (W)
46. Buckboard to Dickinson (JBH)
46. Dickinson Train Depot (DMC)
50. Cabin #2 photo (JBH)
51. Cabin #2 floorplan (JBH)
55. Buffalo Bill's Wild West Show (LOC)
55. Sitting Bull and Buffalo Bill Cody (LOC)
57. Sitting Bull in warbonnet (LOC)
59. Horse "Rico" - gifted to Sitting Bull by Buffalo Bill Cody (North
    Dakota State Historical Society and Standing Rock Sioux, Arcadia
    Books)
61. Cheyenne Indians using a travois 1890 (W)

61. Lakota cradleboard (Metropolitan Museum of Art, NY, NY)

61. Woman from Ute tribe with baby in cradleboard (LOC)

63. Sioux camp (LOC)

63. Lakota moccasins (The American Frontier, William C. Davis, Smithmark, NY, NY)

66, 67. Map of Sitting Bull's Travels (by Dell Radcliffe and Scott Stouffer)

71. Pipe sold to George Dell by Sitting Bull (JBH)

73. Dickinson 1882 (DMC)

84. Baby big-horn sheep (W)

85. Grinding wheel (LOC)

86. Knife gifted by Sitting Bull to George Dell (JBH)

89. Captain George Sword, Chief of Pine Ridge Reservation Agency Police, SD (LOC)

91. Sioux Chiefs in Washington, DC (LOC)

94. Men branding calves (LOC)

95. Cowboy campsite (DMC)

98. Depletion of the Great Sioux Reservation (W: Kmusser)

99. Photo of Sitting Bull presented to Elizabeth Dell (JBH)

100. Lizzie Dell's tin button box (photo by author)

101. Corral in Montana (LOC)

104. Butte where Carl Dell was buried ½ mile from the ranch cabin (photo by author)

117. Dell farm house near Cresco, Iowa, circa 1903 (JBH)

Use the QR code to check out this short video showing the Dell Family Farm, 1935.

The Ice Cube Press began publishing in 1991 to focus on how to live with the natural world and to better understand how people can best live together in the communities they share and inhabit. Using the literary arts to explore life and experiences in the heartland of the United States we have been recognized by a number of well-known writers including: Bill Bradley, Gary Snyder, Gene Logsdon, Wes Jackson, Patricia Hampl, Greg Brown, Jim Harrison, Annie Dillard, Ken Burns, Roz Chast, Jane Hamilton, Daniel Menaker, Kathleen Norris, Janisse Ray, Craig Lesley, Alison Deming, Harriet Lerner, Richard Lynn Stegner, Richard Rhodes, Michael Pollan, David Abram, David Orr, and Barry Lopez. We've published a number of well-known authors including: Mary Swander, Jim Heynen, Mary Pipher, Bill Holm, Connie Mutel, John T. Price, Carol Bly, Marvin Bell, Debra Marquart, Ted Kooser, Stephanie Mills, Bill McKibben, Craig Lesley, Elizabeth McCracken, Derrick Jensen, Dean Bakopoulos, Rick Bass, Linda Hogan, Pam Houston, and Paul Gruchow. Check out Ice Cube Press books on our web site, join our email list, Facebook group, or follow us on Twitter. Visit booksellers, museum shops, or any place you can find good books and support our truly honest to goodness independent publishing projects and discover why we continue striving to "hear the other side."

Ice Cube Press, LLC (Est. 1991)
North Liberty, Iowa, Midwest, USA
Resting above the Silurian and Jordan aquifers
steve@icecubepress.com
Check us out on twitter and facebook
www.icecubepress.com

To Fenna Marie
No questions need be asked
I'm your friend until the end of time.